OXFORD
UNIVERSITY PRESS

T0310314

ASPIRE
SUCCEED
PROGRESS

exam SUCCESS

(in)

BUSINESS STUDIES

for Cambridge IGCSE® & O Level

OXFORD
UNIVERSITY PRESS

Great Clarendon Street, Oxford, OX2 6DP, United Kingdom

Oxford University Press is a department of the University of Oxford. It furthers the University's objective of excellence in research, scholarship, and education by publishing worldwide. Oxford is a registered trade mark of Oxford University Press in the UK and in certain other countries

British Library Cataloguing in Publication Data
Data available

978-0-19-844472-5

1 3 5 7 9 10 8 6 4 2

Paper used in the production of this book is a natural, recyclable product made from wood grown in sustainable forests.
The manufacturing process conforms to the environmental regulations of the country of origin.

Printed in Great Britain by CPI Group (UK) Ltd., Croydon CR0 4YY

Acknowledgements

The publisher and author would like to thank the following for permission to use photographs and other copyright material:

Cover: by Sergey Nivens/Shutterstock

Illustrations: by Aptara.

Photos: p78 (T): CHASSENET / BSIP / Alamy Stock Photo; p78 (MT): happymay / Shutterstock; p78 (MB): Q28 / Alamy Stock Photo; p78 (B): Patti McConville / Alamy Stock Photo; p82 (T): Paul Prescott/ Shutterstock; p82 (B): Ollo/iStockphoto; p88 (T): Brian Titley (author); p88 (M): Natursports / Shutterstock; p88 (B): Tetra Images / Alamy Stock Photo; p103 (T): Mevans/iStockphoto; p103 (B): Ali Ali/EPA/Shutterstock; p116 (T): Art Directors & TRIP / Alamy Stock Photo; p116 (B): MARKUS SCHREIBER/AP/Shutterstock; p137 (TL): Rainer Plendl/Shutterstock; p137 (TR): Dary423/Dreamstime; p137 (BL): Brian Titley (author); p137 (BR): Eric Gevaert/Shutterstock; p159: Thinglass / Shutterstock.

Although we have made every effort to trace and contact all copyright holders before publication this has not been possible in all cases. If notified, the publisher will rectify any errors or omissions at the earliest opportunity.

IGCSE® is the registered trademark of Cambridge Assessment International Education. All examination-style questions and answers within this publication have been written by the authors. In examination, the way marks are awarded may be different.

Contents

Contents

Answers for all
exam-style questions
are available at
www.oxfordsecondary.
com/esg-for-caie-igcse

Matched to the latest Cambridge assessment criteria, this in-depth Exam Success Guide brings clarity and focus to exam preparation with detailed and practical guidance on raising attainment in IGCSE® & O Level Business Studies.

This Exam Success Guide:

- is fully matched to the latest Cambridge IGCSE® & O Level syllabus
- includes comprehensive recap and review features which focus on key course content
- equips you to raise your grade with sample responses and examiner commentary
- will help you to understand exam expectations and avoid common mistakes with examiner tips
- applies knowledge and tests understanding via exam-style questions, with answers available online.

This Exam Success Guide has been designed to summarise the key revision points within each topic to maximise the chance of success in examinations.

Key features include:

- **You need to know:** objectives at the start of each unit to focus your learning

- **Apply:** targeted revision activities are written specifically for this guide, which will help you to apply your knowledge in the exam paper. These provide a variety of transferrable exam skills and techniques. By using a variety of revision styles you'll be able to cement your revision.

- **Recap:** key information and summaries of learning points.

- **Review:** throughout each section, you can review different aspects of the exam with these prompts.

- **Exam tips:** include particular emphasis on content and skills where students commonly struggle. These tips give details on how to maximise marks in the exam.

- **Worked examples:** exemplar questions and answers based on topics.

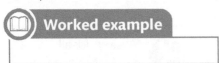

- **Raise your grade:** can be found at the end of the book (Unit 7). This section includes answers from candidates who didn't achieve maximum marks and advice on how to improve answers.

How you will be assessed?

General guidance

Each question is based on one or more of the four assessment objectives: AO1 – AO4.

The amount of marks allocated to each question is clearly marked in brackets. This can be used as a guide to the level of response required.

If the question is only worth two or three marks, then only AO1 and AO2 will be required. If there are 8 or more marks, AO3 is generally required.

12 mark questions will require AO4. Make sure you read the question and the amount of marks allocated thoroughly.

There are two exams for the Business Studies IGCSE® & O Level, each with a slightly different focus.

Paper 1 exam

The Paper 1 exam is 1 hour 30 minutes long and is worth 50% of the total marks.

This paper is a mix of Short Answer and Data Response. There are four questions, each based on a short case study.

Each question is worth 20 marks and focuses on a different section of the syllabus.

There are 80 marks in total. You must answer every question fully.

This exam is externally assessed–make sure that your answers are clear and legible.

Paper 2 exam

The Paper 2 exam is also 1 hour 30 minutes long and is worth 50% of the total marks.

All four questions are based on evidence from one extended case study, supplied in an insert.

Each question is worth 20 marks and focuses on a different section of the syllabus.

There are 80 marks in total. You must answer every question fully.

This exam is externally assessed and you must make sure that your answers are clear and legible.

Exam preparation

To help you prepare for the exam, this book:
- gives you all you need to know about each component
- helps you to understand what is required in different types of question
- helps you to improve your skills for each component to raise your grades
- gives you practice in answering exam-style questions.

Introduction

This Exam Success Guide is designed to bring together all the most important elements of your IGCSE® & O Level Business Studies course and help you in planning your revision.

With a clear focus on the necessary subject content and vocabulary, this guide should help you to organise your study timetable and have clear, bite-size pieces of revision. Each unit includes revision questions that will test your knowledge and skills. Worked examples and exam tips highlight the ways in which you should approach different types of questions and set out your answers.

However you look at it, revision can be boring! But, whatever revision you do should be **active**. This page will help you develop useful ways of revising.

Revising in groups

Working as a group is always better than alone. Try these ideas out.

Form a study group with friends. Join with two or three friends and fix times when you'll go through key topics. Do timed questions together, then mark them. Make lists of things you don't understand to ask your teacher.

Working together at home. Message, Facetime or Skype friends and test each other. Go through questions together.

Know your key words. Make lists of key words that you need to know.

Test each other. Make flash cards of key words and have revision competitions.

Revising in class

You'll have lessons to revise topics that you're not clear about. Use the time well!

Get to know question styles. Know command words, practise timed answers and plan longer extended answers.

Get to know how exam questions are marked.

Look at past answers. Some exam boards publish model answers, or have marking exercises as part of their training for teachers. Go through these, so that you know how examiners mark.

Extra lessons. Make lists of questions about things you don't understand about past exam questions, then see your teacher to go through them.

Ask your teacher for revision help. Your teacher can give you questions on particular topics you are less confident about.

Revising alone

At some stage, you'll have to revise alone! Don't sit in front of the TV trying to read notes that you're not sure about! Try these variations.

> Act on weaknesses. Make a checklist of things you need to know, similar to those in the unit introductions in this book

> Watch video clips from YouTube, or other websites. Allow no more than 15 minutes, which is as long as most people can concentrate fully.

> Work on past exam papers. The more papers you try, the more familiar you'll be with examiners' style.

Making a revision timetable

Revision doesn't just happen – for it to go well, it needs to be well planned! Here are some handy hints to help you plan.

> Two to three months before exams begin, draw up a revision timetable.

> Draw up a plan for your school holidays.

> Divide up the time between the subjects and topics that you need to revise.

> Every revision day during the school holidays has three time slots – morning, afternoon, and evening. Use two of these on each day; give yourself some free time. You should have one day and at least two evenings that are completely free in your timetable.

> Split the three time slots into three 50-minute chunks.

Three stages of revision

The worst thing you can do is to stare at a book of notes! Be **active** about revising and the time will fly past. Split your time up into 50-minute chunks and use the table below to help you plan what to do.

Stage 1 Mending the gaps in your knowledge and understanding	Select a topic you're unclear about, where there are gaps (perhaps you missed work) or which you find more difficult. • Read through the topic you want to revise using your own work and also the Exam Success Guide. • Make a list of key words. • Write a definition of each key word. Use your notes and the Exam Success Guide or Student Book to help.

Stage 2A Revising uncertain topics The first 50 minutes	Select a topic you're becoming clearer about. • Read through the topic you want to revise using your own work and also the Exam Success Guide. • As you read, copy sub-headings on a sheet of file paper, and leave gaps ready for some notes. • In the gaps, write out questions about the topic as though you were an examiner.
Stage 2B Becoming more confident	Go back to your headings, questions and spaces. • Now fill in answers to questions as far as you can, without looking at notes or your Exam Success Guide. Don't worry about the ones you can't answer. • When you finish you can see at a glance what you know and what you don't know. • For any gaps, go back and look at your notes and Exam Success Guide. Then do the questions again. • Read through any past exam questions or practice questions that you've been given and make a list of the topics you think you know well.
Before Stage 3	List your strong and weak topics based upon marks in tests, and gaps in your understanding from the stages above. Be honest about your strengths and weaknesses!

Stage 3 Revising topics fully	Focus on the topics you now know well in your revision timetable. • Try the practice questions from your Exam Success Guide or Student Book. • Either self-assess using the mark schemes, or peer mark questions done by friends using the mark scheme. • Hand in your practice question answers to your teacher for marking. • Review.

Unit 1:
Understanding business activity

Unit outline

Unit 1 will introduce you to the key ideas of business activity in the IGCSE® & O Level Complete Business Studies textbook, making sure that you are able to utilize all of your learning.

This unit will highlight the key areas of learning and condense the key facts and basic analysis points you will need for your exam.

Your revision checklist

Either tick these boxes to build a record of your revision, *or* use them to identify your strengths and weaknesses.

Specification	Theme	☺	☺	☹
1.1 Business activity	1.1.1 What is business activity?			
	1.1.2 Specialization			
1.2 Classification of businesses	1.2.1 Business sectors			
	1.2.2 Mixed economies			
1.3 Enterprise, business growth and business failure	1.3.1 Entrepreneurs and entrepreneurship			
	1.3.2 Measuring business size			
	1.3.3 Business growth			
	1.3.4 Small business			
	1.3.5 Business failure			
1.4 Types of business organization	1.4.1 Main types of private sector business organization			
	1.4.2 Business organizations in the public sector			
1.5 Business objectives and stakeholder objectives	1.5.1 The importance of business objectives			
	1.5.2 Stakeholder groups and their objectives			

- the purpose and nature of business activity
- the role of specialization.

 Recap

Business activity involves organizing, combining and using **scarce resources** to satisfy the **needs** and **wants** of the **consumer**.

1.1.1 What is business activity?

The public and private sectors

Most **private sector** businesses have the aim of making a **profit** by producing and selling a good or service that the consumer needs or wants. If a private sector business cannot make a profit, then the business will not have enough capital left to reinvest or pay the owner a wage.

Some private sector businesses do not have the aim of making a profit. Other objectives include:

- helping others – charities aim to help people, animals or the natural environment and are often funded through donations and gifts

- provide services to members – in the cases of social or sports clubs, membership fees are used to keep the clubs operating with no profit.

Most **public sector** businesses do not have the aim of making a profit. Instead, they provide public services free of charge (e.g. health care, police and fire services). These services are paid for through **taxes**.

The four factors of production

Entrepreneurs use the four factors of production (see Figure 1.1) to produce the goods and services required by consumers to meet their **organizational goals**.

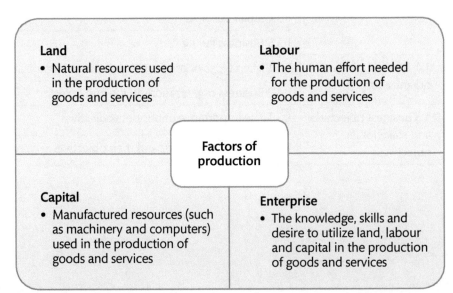

Land
- Natural resources used in the production of goods and services

Labour
- The human effort needed for the production of goods and services

Factors of production

Capital
- Manufactured resources (such as machinery and computers) used in the production of goods and services

Enterprise
- The knowledge, skills and desire to utilize land, labour and capital in the production of goods and services

Figure 1.1 *The four factors of production influence the entrepreneur's choices and chances of success in business*

The entrepreneur will be able to earn a profit if the business is successful.

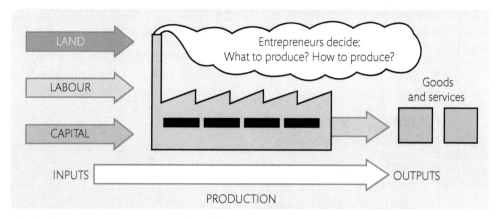

Figure 1.2 *Resources are organized into firms to produce goods and services*

Figure 1.2 shows the process an entrepreneur will go through to produce goods and services. As supplies of the four factors of production are always limited, the entrepreneur must make choices about the best combination to use. Making these choices always involves risking resources, and decisions involve a mixture of planning, research and instinct.

Successful entrepreneurs will choose the option which makes the best use of resources and helps achieve business objectives.

1.1.2 Specialization

As we live in a modern trading society, businesses and entrepreneurs make the most efficient use of their available factors of production and trade for goods and services that they cannot produce themselves.

The most important reasons trade and specialization have flourished are:

- the use of money as a method of exchanging goods and services

- specialized machinery, which has improved the quality and quantity of goods and services produced

- the **automation** of this machinery

- international specialization based on available raw materials in a given country or region.

Specialization has led to the division of labour, where individual people and machines complete the same task over and over again. Below are some of the main advantages and disadvantages of labour **specialization**.

 Recap

It is important to ensure that the opportunity cost of your business is minimal and that you make the best use of your factors of production. Specialization is one way of achieving this.

Advantages of labour specialization	Disadvantages of labour specialization
✓ Employees can make best use of their particular talents and skills. ✓ Employees can increase their skills and experience by repeating tasks. ✓ Employees can produce more output and reduce business costs if they concentrate on the same job or tasks. ✓ More productive employees can earn higher wages.	✗ Individuals must rely on others to produce the goods and services they want but cannot produce themselves. ✗ Workers can become bored doing the same job or completing repetitive tasks. The quality and efficiency of their work may fall. ✗ Many repetitive manual tasks are now undertaken by computer-controlled machinery and robots. This has reduced job satisfaction for many workers and reduced employment opportunities for many low-skilled workers.

Entrepreneurs make profits by **adding value** to their good and services, which they do by satisfying customer needs and wants.

If an entrepreneur is unable to add any value to their product, consumers will not want to buy it. There will be no sales and therefore no profits will be made.

 Worked example

Identify two features of a public sector organization. (2)

Public sector organizations:
- are controlled by the government
- do not usually aim to make a profit.

 Apply

Create a set of domino cards. On one half of the card, write 'public' or 'private'. On the other half, have a feature associated with a public or privately-owned business. Practice matching the two halves in a game of dominoes.

 Review

Before you continue, make sure you are able to define and give examples of:
- business activity and the main aims of business
- entrepreneurs, opportunity cost and specialization
- business activity in the public and private sector.

You need to know:
- the different types of business sectors
- the difference between the public and private sector.

1.2.1 Business sectors

The primary, secondary and tertiary sectors

Job roles fall into a specific business sector:

- **Raw materials** are collected in the **primary sector**.

- Businesses process raw materials into goods for sale in the **secondary sector**. A business may sell its goods to another business, which puts together many products ready for sale to the final customer.

- The **tertiary sector** consists of businesses that sell finished goods to the final customer.

Figure 1.3 shows the processes involved in the production of bread.

◀◀ Recap

As mentioned in the previous unit, businesses often specialize. This often leads to businesses doing one of three jobs:

- growing or gathering raw materials

- processing raw materials into a finished product

- providing a service by selling the product to the final user.

Figure 1.3 *A chain of production for bread*

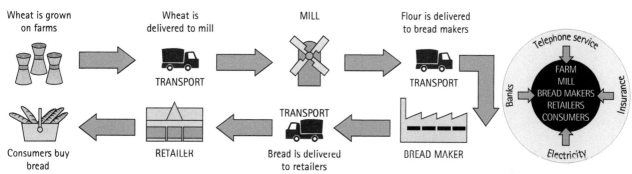

📖 Worked example

State and explain two reasons why there are many stages in the secondary sector of bread production. (4)

Because:

- each stage specializes in one specific factor, such as milling, which makes each process quicker

- one stage can deliver to many customers, which reduces the fixed cost of production.

✏️ Apply

Can you separate the stages of bread production into primary, secondary and tertiary sectors?

Choose other businesses and see if you can separate the processes involved.

Exam tip

On Paper 1, any question worth four marks or more and all questions on Paper 2 require application to a case study – make sure to read any stimulus material carefully and highlight key areas to focus on.

◀◀ Recap

Primary, secondary and tertiary businesses make up the **economy** of a country. Each country has a different mix of primary, secondary and tertiary businesses depending on a number of factors, including:

- availability of raw materials

- level of industrialization

- average income level.

Sectors in developing and developed countries

Countries with less developed economies often rely heavily on the primary sector – such as agriculture or mining – for their economy.

Newly industrialized/developing countries often rely less on the primary sector and focus more on the secondary sector.

Developed countries often **de-industrialize** and focus business activities more on services in the tertiary sector.

1.2.2 Mixed economies

This term refers to the mix of public and private sector organizations.

Public sector organizations include:

- national, regional and local government authorities that look after the general running of the country
- government agencies that look after specific services
- public corporations that are business-like and carry out public sector tasks necessary for society to function properly.

> **Recap**
>
> Public sector organizations provide the goods and services that consumers *need*, those that private sector firms are unwilling or unable to produce. There is usually little or no competition.
>
> Public corporations may produce a profit, however these profits will be reinvested into the service, or into another public sector service.

Private sector organizations include:

- **sole traders**
- **partnerships**
- **limited companies.**

Private sector organizations usually aim to make a profit for their owners by providing products or services that consumers *want*. These products or services are usually profitable. Any profits will be reinvested or taken by the owner as a reward for success.

There is usually competition between businesses to attract as many consumers as possible. A successful business will be able to maximize profits if there is high demand and low competition.

> **Review**
>
> Before you continue, make sure you are able to:
>
> - classify and give examples of business activity within the primary, secondary and tertiary sectors
> - classify and give examples of business enterprises within the public and private sector
> - explain why the public sector needs to provide services the private sector is unwilling or unable to provide.

Exam tip

A common mistake in exams is to discuss public limited companies when asked about public sector companies, and vice versa – make sure you can remember the difference between the two.

Exam tip

Franchises are not an example of a private sector organization. Franchising is a method of business ownership in which a large company authorizes a smaller company or individual to carry out commercial activity under its name.

You need to know:
- the difference between enterprise and entrepreneurship
- the methods and problems associated with measuring business size
- why some businesses grow and others remain small
- why some businesses fail.

1.3.1 Entrepreneurs and entrepreneurship

Entrepreneurs

A person who starts their own **enterprise** is called an **entrepreneur**. There are many advantages and disadvantages to being an entrepreneur.

The characteristics of an entrepreneur include an ability to:

- organize and manage the production of goods and services effectively
- calculate the **opportunity cost** of using scarce resources
- manage and take business risks
- motivate themselves to work hard independently.

Advantages of being an entrepreneur	Disadvantages of being an entrepreneur
✓ **Making best use of your skills and interests:** running and owning your own business can be more satisfying than working in a job that is dull and repetitive.	✗ **Increased risk:** many new businesses fail within their first few years resulting in their owners losing the capital they invested in them.
✓ **Being independent:** being able to take decisions, for example, about the hours you work and who you want to work with, rather than being told what to do by an employer.	✗ **Increased responsibility:** for taking all the decisions necessary to run and manage a business and possibly also for managing employees.
✓ **Increased motivation:** from being able to put your own ideas into practice, taking big decisions that will affect your future and being rewarded with profit if your business venture is successful.	✗ **Long hours:** business owners often have to work very long hours and, if there is no one else to help them, they will lose revenues and profits if they take time off for holidays or when they are ill.
✓ **The potential to earn more income:** by working hard to make your business successful and profitable.	✗ **High opportunity cost:** the loss of a steady income from regular paid employment.

Entrepreneurship

Entrepreneurship is the act of setting up a business by an entrepreneur.

Entrepreneurship consists of more than just setting up a business. An entrepreneur must go through many stages in order to be successful.

⏪ Recap

Most businesses start very small, with a sole trader. This person has often decided to take a risk by working this way (often referred to as 'working for yourself').

Exam tip

A sole trader does not always work alone; a sole trader may have employees, but the sole trader is the only decision maker.

✎ Apply

Make two sets of flash cards with the characteristics of entrepreneurs on one and aspects of entrepreneurship on the other. You can then use these to revise by playing snap and matching characteristics.

Business plans

The most important stage of setting up a business is planning. This usually consists of a **business plan** that contains the following sections:

- the aims and objectives of the business
- a description of the goods and/or services on offer
- the market potential for the goods and services
- a plan for production
- how the resources will be allocated
- a financial plan consisting of costs, revenue and profit
- details of sources of **finance**.

Drafting a comprehensive business plan has a number of benefits.
A business plan will allow the entrepreneur to:

- assess the possibility of turning a business idea into a successful business
- set out short-, medium- and long-term goals to achieve the **business objectives**
- support an application for financial help
- monitor performance against the plan
- revise the business objectives over time (see Figure 1.4).

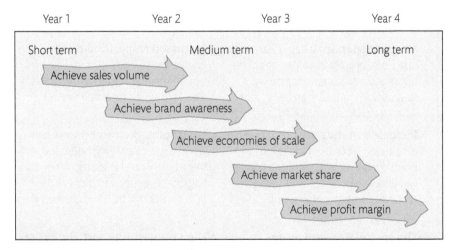

Figure 1.4 *Business objectives may change over time*

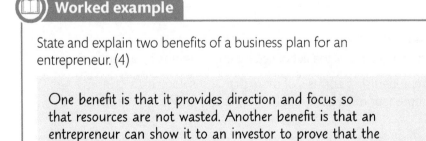

Worked example

State and explain two benefits of a business plan for an entrepreneur. (4)

> One benefit is that it provides direction and focus so that resources are not wasted. Another benefit is that an entrepreneur can show it to an investor to prove that the business idea can be successful.

1.3.2 Measuring business size

Businesses are usually either large enterprises or small-to-medium enterprises (SMEs). It is important to know the size of the business so stakeholders can make decisions that affect the future of the business.

Why is it useful to measure the size of firms?

The following **stakeholders** (groups of people and organizations with an interest in businesses) may want to compare the size of different firms and monitor whether they are growing or shrinking in size over time.

- **Business owners** may want to know the size of rival firms they compete with.

- **Investors** will want to make a good return on the money they invest in different businesses.

- **Banks** will want to know whether a firm is big enough to take out a loan and make repayments.

- **Trade unions** and other organizations representing workers will want to know how many workers firms employ.

- **Consumers** or consumer representatives may be concerned about the power some large firms have over prices and the quality of goods and services.

- **Government officials** may want to encourage the creation and growth of small firms to compete with large firms and may set different tax rates on the profits of large and small businesses.

It is important to use the most appropriate measure of size for a business – a business which is very large may employ few people or have a small amount of capital employed. If you use the wrong measure then the stakeholder may not have all of the information necessary to make informed decisions.

Measure	Limitations
Number of employees How many employees work for the business? Fewer than 50 employees is usually a small business.	Some businesses are capital intensive, especially in the technology sector or where production processes are automated.
Capital employed The money (capital) invested by the owners' personal funds in machinery, buildings, materials and cash that is held to acquire resources.	Labour-intensive firms may use huge amounts of labour but have few assets.
Output or sales Comparing the value of a business output in relation to competitors in the same industry. Output is related to the number of products produced in a period of time. Sales is related to the revenue earnt by a business in a period of time.	It is difficult to compare between different industries, as there are so many variables. A small baker may produce many thousands of loaves of bread, but still be smaller than a shipbuilder making one ship a month.
Market share The proportion of revenue or output of the total market attributed to one business.	Not all markets are large – a small business with a monopoly in a small town could have a huge market share.

Exam tip

Think carefully about the type of examples given in your exam – not all methods of measuring business size will be relevant to the question.

1.3.3 Business growth

As businesses become more established, there is often pressure to grow the size of the business to capitalize on its success. Some of the main reasons are shown in the table below:

Cost advantages	Increase sales/profits/market share	Increase access to funds	Diversification	Increase in responsibilities and salaries
Bulk buying raw materials may reduce the unit cost and/or increased output may reduce fixed costs per unit: **economies of scale**	Increased sales may increase the brand image and, along with the cost advantages, may increase profits and market share: **growth**	Banks and investors are often more willing to invest in larger business with lower rates of interest, as these businesses are seen as less risky: **access to finance**	As a business becomes more successful it will have more retained earnings that can be used for investing in newer machinery and/or expanding into different areas: **diversification**	As businesses grow larger they earn higher profits which can be shared between workers and owners: **increased profits**

 Worked example

Explain two advantages of growing the size of a business. (2)

> Gaining economies of scale and the opportunity for increased profits.

Exam tip

Remember that every time you give an example you must explain it to get the full marks available.

Methods of business growth

There are two methods in which businesses can grow: internal and external.

Internal growth

Expanding operations (scale of production)

Financed by:
- Retained profits
- Loans from banks and lenders
- Share capital from investors

External growth

Integration with other businesses

Examples include:
- Merger – when two or more businesses agree to join and form a larger business
- Takeover (aquisition) – buying enough shares of another business to take control of its operations (with or without agreement)

Worked example

What is meant by external growth? (2)

> External growth means integrating with other businesses by mergers or takeovers.

When a business pursues external growth, there are three **integration** strategies a business can use, depending on what it wants to achieve. These are horizontal, vertical and lateral integration (see Figure 1.5).

Figure 1.5a Horizontal integration

Figure 1.5b Vertical integration

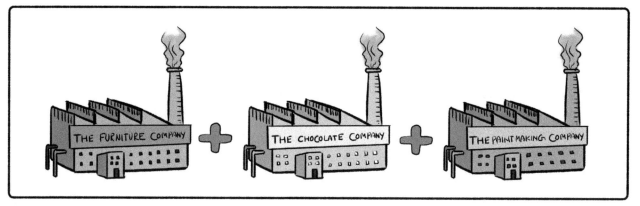

Figure 1.5c Lateral integration

Apply

Choose a business and then challenge a friend to identify how this business may grow horizontally, vertically and laterally.

1.3.4 Small business

Although there are many small entrepreneurial businesses, only a small number grow, while most stay small. In some cases, businesses may choose to stay small (see Figure 1.6).

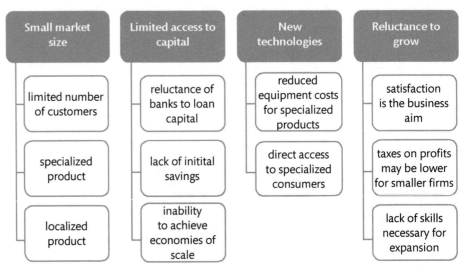

Small market size	Limited access to capital	New technologies	Reluctance to grow
limited number of customers	reluctance of banks to loan capital	reduced equipment costs for specialized products	satisfaction is the business aim
specialized product	lack of initital savings	direct access to specialized consumers	taxes on profits may be lower for smaller firms
localized product	inability to achieve economies of scale		lack of skills necessary for expansion

Figure 1.6 *Business expansion does not necessarily mean success; there are many reasons a business might want to stay small*

Access to resources	Managing operations over large areas	Inability to attract skilled employees
• scarcity of resources • larger businesses may achieve better purchasing economies	• difficulties in managing multiple locations • merging different businesses, locations and/or cultures	• lack of employees with the appropriate skills • employees may want to work for established companies • high training costs

Figure 1.7 *When businesses attempt growth, there are many potential problems that need to be overcome if the business is to succeed*

Apply

Write a leaflet for an entrepreneur explaining the types of support that may be available.

Government support for small businesses

Governments support entrepreneurs for many reasons, including to:

* reduce unemployment

* encourage social enterprise

* increase competition

* boost economic growth.

However, not all enterprises are given support by governments, as governments have limited finances. Support may be dependent on:

* the amount of jobs a new business may create

* the amount of capital invested by the entrepreneur

* whether the type of business will add value to the national economy

* the planning and preparation of the entrepreneur.

The government may support businesses using the methods shown in Figure 1.8.

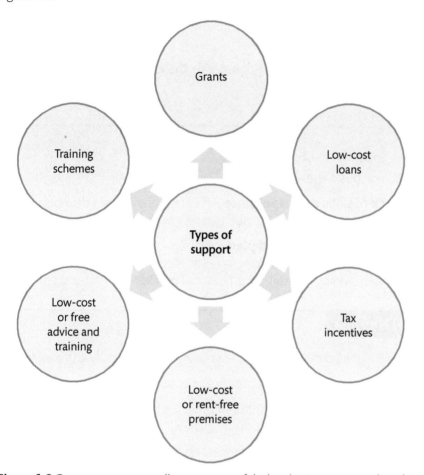

Figure 1.8 *Governments are usually more successful when businesses succeed, so they may provide additional support*

 **Review**

Before you continue, make sure you are able to:

* understand and explain what an entrepreneur is, and the concept of entrepreneurship

* describe the characteristics of successful entrepreneurs

* list the contents of a business plan and how they assist entrepreneurs

* explain why and how governments provide support for business **start-ups**.

1.3.5 Business failure

Reasons for **business failure** may include:

Lack of management skills	• A skilled tradesperson does not always know how to manage resources including employees and raw materials. • As businesses expand, tasks which are simple on a small scale grow to be more complex as the size of the business increases.
Changes in the business environment	• The economy can move from boom to recession (or vice versa), which can change the number of consumers. • Consumer preferences may change with new fashions and trends. • The loss of a vital customer or supplier may leave a business unable to be financially viable. • Increased competition may decrease prices and profits. • Laws and regulations may change, imposing additional costs on a business.
Liquidity problems	• As businesses expand, finance is needed for expansion. If there is poor cash flow then although the business may be viable, there is not enough cash available to continue trading.

Exam tip

Many businesses may have high sales, but if their cash flow is poor then the business may still fail.

 Recap

Although many businesses fail at the introductory stage, established businesses can also fail. Many of the reasons for **failure** are similar for both established and new businesses.

Worked example

Identify two causes of business failure. (2)

> Liquidity problems and changes to the external business environment.

New business failure

Most new businesses fail for two specific reasons:

1. **Lack of skills and experience** – If entrepreneurs start new businesses, they often make mistakes due to a lack of knowledge,

2. **Failure to research and plan** – Without effective research and planning, a business is likely to fail as there may be a lack of understanding regarding the potential **market** size and costs involved.

 Review

Before you continue, make sure you are able to identify and explain:

*   the concepts and characteristics of enterprise and entrepreneurship
*   how business plans assist entrepreneurs in creating enterprises and gaining government support
*   methods and problems of measuring business size
*   why some businesses grow and others remain small
*   the causes of business failure.

 Apply

Read the newspapers and try to explain any current external pressures that may currently affect businesses.

You need to know:
- the main features of different business organizational forms.

1.4.1 Main types of private sector business organization

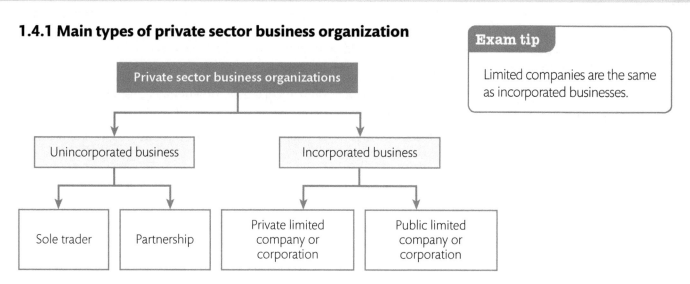

Each type of business organization has different legal and procedural elements.

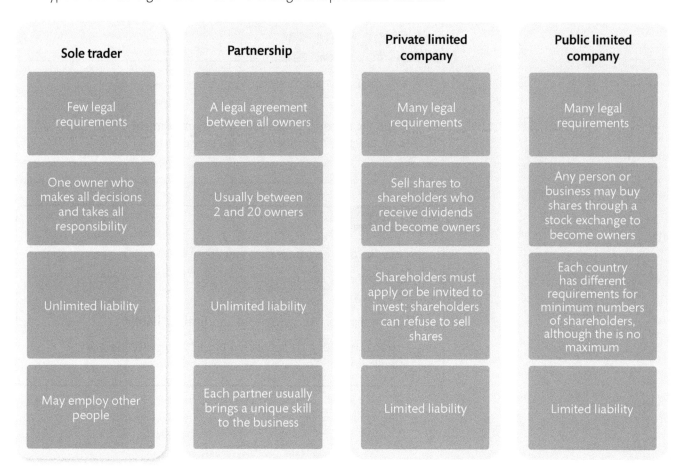

Sole trader	Partnership	Private limited company	Public limited company
Few legal requirements	A legal agreement between all owners	Many legal requirements	Many legal requirements
One owner who makes all decisions and takes all responsibility	Usually between 2 and 20 owners	Sell shares to shareholders who receive dividends and become owners	Any person or business may buy shares through a stock exchange to become owners
Unlimited liability	Unlimited liability	Shareholders must apply or be invited to invest; shareholders can refuse to sell shares	Each country has different requirements for minimum numbers of shareholders, although the is no maximum
May employ other people	Each partner usually brings a unique skill to the business	Limited liability	Limited liability

1.4.2 Business organizations in the public sector

Business organizations in the public sector differ from those in the private sector, as the main objective is not to make a profit and there are no **shareholders**.

Most business organizations in the public sector have been **nationalized** – taken out of private ownership and the main aim is to provide a product or service that would be unprofitable for a private business organization.

There are three main types of public business organizations:

- those which focus on particular government functions, such as the central bank

- those which provide essential public services like police, fire and health services

- those which provide commercial activities, such as state-owned rail companies.

 Apply

identify which public sector organizations are in your country and categorize them into a type of public organization.

 Worked example

What is meant by 'public sector'? (2)

> The public sector is controlled by the government AND paid for by taxes OR provides essential services.

 Review

Before you continue, make sure you are able to:

- identify and explain the different types of business organization and their features

- the concepts of risk, ownership and **limited liability**

- explain the difference between a public and private sector organization.

Exam tip

Although it is not the main aim of the public sector to make a profit, if a public organization does make a profit, it is reinvested into public services, not given as a dividend to shareholders.

- that businesses and stakeholders can have several objectives and their importance my change
- the role of stakeholder groups involved in business activity
- the differences between the objectives of private and public sector enterprises.

1.5.1 The importance of business objectives

A **business objective** is a goal or aim a business wants to achieve that gives a purpose and direction for the organization and its employees.

There are short- and long-term business objectives:

- Short-term aims are designed to give specific targets that should be achieved; these are usually **SMART** and are focused on specific departments.

- Long-term aims are strategic and require less detail. These aims are general guidance for all departments within a business, such as a **mission statement**.

> **Exam tip**
>
> Short term aims are usually SMART – **S**pecific, **M**easurable, **A**chievable, **R**ealistic, **T**ime-based – make sure you understand this concept.

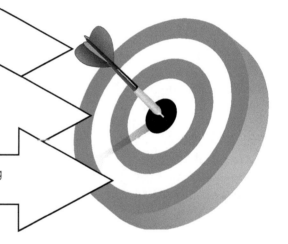

A clear set of goals for owners, managers and employees to work together to achieve

A focus for planning what the business needs to do to achieve these goals

A way of measuring business performance over time by assessing how close or far the business is from achieving them

Figure 1.9 *What business objectives provide*

Types of business objectives

The most common business objectives in the private sector are:

- Survival – Often the first and most important objective of most new businesses. This may have a specific focus, such as achieving positive cash flow or gaining a consumer base.

- Profitability – The ability to sell their products and services at a price that is higher than the cost of delivery. This may be either profit satisficing or profit maximization.

- Growth – To increase the size of their, consumer base, sales, market share and/or profits. Benefits of growth include greater economies of scale and a reduction of business risk.

- Increased market share – to gain a larger percentage of the total market by providing goods and services that are more desirable than a business competitor.

> **Exam tip**
>
> Many students confuse the term 'stakeholder' with 'shareholder' – make sure that you are confident in your definitions and use them appropriately.

Worked example

What is meant by 'survival'? (2)

> This is an objective of most businesses; to remain competitive and/or profitable in the market.

Why business objectives may change over time

Aims and objectives are set as targets for specific stakeholders. Once an aim or objective is achieved, it no longer serves a purpose and must be replaced.

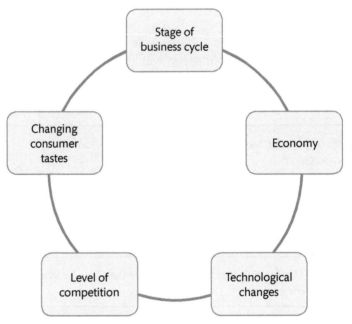

Figure 1.10 *There are several factors which mean business objectives must be changed or replaced*

◀◀ **Recap**

There are also external influences that mean a business must react and change its objective in order to meet its short-term or immediate needs. A number of common external influences are shown in Figure 1.10.

Exam tip

A social enterprise is not a form of business ownership, it is a business objective.

Objectives of social enterprises

A **social enterprise** prioritizes social needs and environmental issues over shareholder **dividends**. Although social enterprises aim to make a profit, not all of these profits are used for reinvestment for growth or shareholder dividends – social enterprises aim to maximize well-being and sustainability.

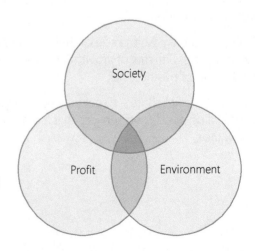

Figure 1.11 *A successful social enterprise must manage a different set of priorities to a private sector business*

1.5.2 Stakeholder groups and their objectives

A stakeholder is a person or group who is affected or can be affected by a particular business or activity within a business.

Stakeholders are affected by the business aims and decisions but can also influence the future direction of a business, depending on the amount of influence the stakeholder group possesses.

There are two types of **stakeholders**: internal and external.

> **Exam tip**
>
> Although managers and employees are both workers, they have different aims and objectives, so are classed as two separate stakeholders.

Internal stakeholders

Owners and shareholders, **managers** and employees are examples of internal stakeholders.

Owners and shareholders	Invest capital and/or time with an expectation of receiving dividends
Managers	Make decisions and aim to meet business objectives by managing resources as effectively as possible
Employees	Produce the goods or provide the services in order to meet the business objectives and receive the best possible income and conditions

External stakeholders

External stakeholders do not play a direct role in a business, but still have expectations and requirements of the business.

Creditors	Those a business has borrowed money or stock from and needs to repay, e.g. suppliers and money lenders
Government	Raises taxes and regulates business activity
Community or society	Depends on the wealth created by a business, and is affected by its impact on the local environment

How stakeholder objectives may conflict

Different stakeholders have different priorities, which means that what may be a positive outcome for one stakeholder is a negative outcome for another, as shown in Figure 1.12.

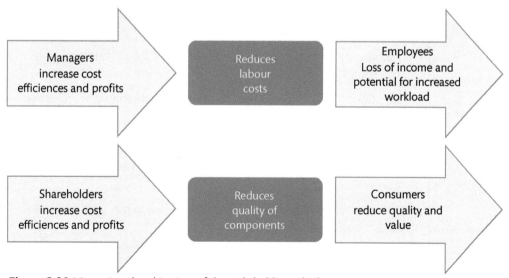

Figure 1.12 *Managing the objectives of the stakeholders, which will always involve compromise, is vital to the success of a business*

Worked example

Identify and explain two ways in which increasing wages might affect a stakeholder in a business. (6)

> Shareholders may be affected as the increase in costs will reduce the profits of the business, which will mean dividends may be lower than expected. Employees may be affected as they will earn higher wages than they were expecting, which may increase motivation and therefore increase the productivity of the business.

Objectives of the public and private sectors

The main concern of the private sector is to make a sustainable profit that is used to meet the objectives of the main stakeholders of the business.

The public sector does not usually have a profit motive; the main objectives for the public sector are not based on profit and may focus on the impact of the public service on society and the environment, as shown in the table below.

Aim	Rationale
To achieve financial targets	As the public sector is financed by taxes, there are strict targets to control and reduce financial costs.
Provide good quality public service	To meet the minimum needs of the population which may not be profitable for the private sector.
Achieve social objectives	The government aims to protect the rights of the general population and ensure that all citizens' basic social needs are met.
Achieve environmental objectives	The government has to lead the way in environmental protection and ensure that private sector businesses respect and look after the environment.

 Review

Before you continue, make sure you are able to:

- identify and explain different business objectives including social objectives
- identify and explain why businesses have more than one objective
- describe and explain the main stakeholder groups involved in business activity and their objectives
- describe and explain how stakeholders' objectives might be in conflict
- demonstrate an ability to differentiate between public and private sector business objectives.

Exam-style questions

Unit 1

Jack and Jill are friends who created a partnership agreement for their business. Jack is a shoemaker and Jill studied design at university. They produce handmade, unique women's shoes using job production. The quality of the design, materials and manufacture are important for Jack and Jill and their customers.

The customers pay premium prices for these unique shoes and often ask for custom designed shoes. As their raw material costs are high, Jill is investigating whether Jack could change to a batch production method to minimize their costs.

(a) What is meant by a 'partnership'? (2)

(b) Identify two advantages to Jack and Jill of using job production. (2)

(c) What is meant by 'job production'? (2)

(d) What is meant by 'batch production'? (2)

(e) Identify two features of a partnership. (2)

(f) Identify two disadvantages Jack and Jill will face when using job production. (2)

(g) Identify two raw materials Jack might use in the production of his shoes. (2)

(h) Identify and explain two disadvantages of producing handmade shoes. (4)

(i) Identify and explain two advantages of producing handmade shoes. (4)

(j) Identify and explain two benefits of changing to a batch production method. (6)

(k) Do you think Jack and Jill should change their production method for the manufacture of shoes? Justify your answer. (6)

(l) Identify and explain two drawbacks of changing to a batch production method. (6)

Exam tip

The exam paper will always ask for the definition of a term found in the case study. However, your answer does not need to be linked to the details found in the case study.

Exam tip

Can you think of any other exam-style questions to set for your friends?

Unit 2:
People in business

Unit outline

While the first chapter investigated **business activity**, this chapter focuses on the people who work in and manage businesses, how they can affect and influence business decisions and legal issues that need to be considered.

Your revision checklist

Either tick these boxes to build a record of your revision, *or* use them to identify your strengths and weaknesses.

Specification	Theme	☺	😐	☹
2.1 Motivating employees	2.1.1 Why do people work?			
	2.1.2 Theories of employee motivation and behaviour			
	2.1.3 Methods of motivation			
2.2 Organization and management	2.2.1 Why do businesses have organizational structures?			
	2.2.2 The role of management			
	2.2.3 Leadership styles			
	2.2.4 Trade unions			
2.3 Recruitment, selection and training	2.3.1 The main stages of recruitment and selection			
	2.3.2 Training			
	2.3.3 Workforce reduction			
	2.3.4 Employment law			
2.4 Internal and external communication	2.4.1 Communication			
	2.4.2 Methods of communication			
	2.4.3 Communication barriers			

You need to know:
- the importance of a well-motivated workforce
- methods of motivation.

2.1.1 Why do people work?

 Worked example

Identify two motivating factors. (2)

Financial motivators and non-financial motivators.

⏪ **Recap**

As people are different, there are many factors that motivate people to work. Some motivators are **financial** and others are **non-financial**.

Most people require a certain level of pay (**wage** or **salary**) to work, which allows them to buy goods and services they need and want. However, while pay can encourage people to go to work, it doesn't always motivate.

But not all people require money, such as volunteers who work at charities. In these cases, other motivators are needed to satisfy the needs of an employee.

What makes a job satisfying?

Factors include:

- good wages and other benefits, pension, company car, etc.
- reasonable hours of work
- generous holiday entitlement
- a safe and clean working environment
- challenging and interesting tasks
- training opportunities
- working as part of a team
- being consulted on management decisions

- opportunities for promotion
- job security
- being trusted to take on new responsibilities
- regular feedback on performance
- bonus payments in recognition of good work
- job status
- good social relationships inside and outside of the workplace with work colleagues.

As shown, there are a lot of motivators that can encourage employees to work hard.

The benefits of a well-motivated workforce

Most **private sector** businesses have the aim of making a **profit** by producing and selling. If a workforce is motivated, there are a number of benefits for the business.

Siemens gives me the opportunity to progress and to learn new things. This makes me feel valued by the company.

I like my work because the company encourages me to think creatively and suggest ways of improving products and processes. Managers recognize my achievements and the best ideas and projects are even rewarded financially.

Increased labour productivity	• Satisfied workers are more likely to work efficiently • Efficiency leads to increased output and profit
Reduced absenteeism	• Happy workers are less likely to take unplanned time off work (e.g. sick days) • Less cover for absent workers reduces costs and increases profits
Reduced labour turnover	• Happy workers will stay with a business, making sure important skills and experience are kept • Reduces recruitment, training and selection time and costs, increasing productivity and profits

Figure 2.1 *Motivated employees are more productive, more reliable, and more loyal*

2.1.2 Theories of employee motivation and behaviour

Maslow's hierarchy of needs

Human needs		Employee needs
Developing your full potential A sense of achivement	Self-actualization	Taking on more responsibility Promotion and development
To feel valued Status and recognition	Esteem needs	Promotion opportunities Positive feedback from managers
Friendship A sense of belonging To gain respect	Social needs	Supportive work colleagues Working as a team Good working relationships
Personal safety Security	Safety and security needs	Job security Safe working environment
Food Clothing Shelter	Physiological needs	Reasonable wage or salary

Figure 2.2 *Maslow's hierarchy of human needs*

Abraham Maslow, a psychologist, believed that employees were essential, and that it was important to meet their psychological as well as their physiological needs, and created a pyramid showing what motivates employees at work to achieve business targets (see Figure 2.2).

Physiological needs (wages) are needed by *most* employees to ensure that they are able to buy the goods and services needed to survive.

Safety needs (contracts and laws) are also necessary for *most* employees so that they do not worry about losing their jobs.

Most employees need to have their **social needs** met (friendship) so that they enjoy going to work.

Fewer employees require their **esteem needs** (respect) to be met. Employees who take pride in their work or want promotions aspire to this need.

Although *many* aspire to **self-actualization,** *few* employees achieve this need.

Exam tip

Not all employees need to have job security or wages. It is possible to travel down the pyramid (e.g. when you lose your job) as well as up.

Taylor's scientific management

Frederick Taylor was an engineer, and had a different approach (see Figure 2.3) in ensuring that business targets were met. Taylor did not trust employees and believed they could only be motivated by money.

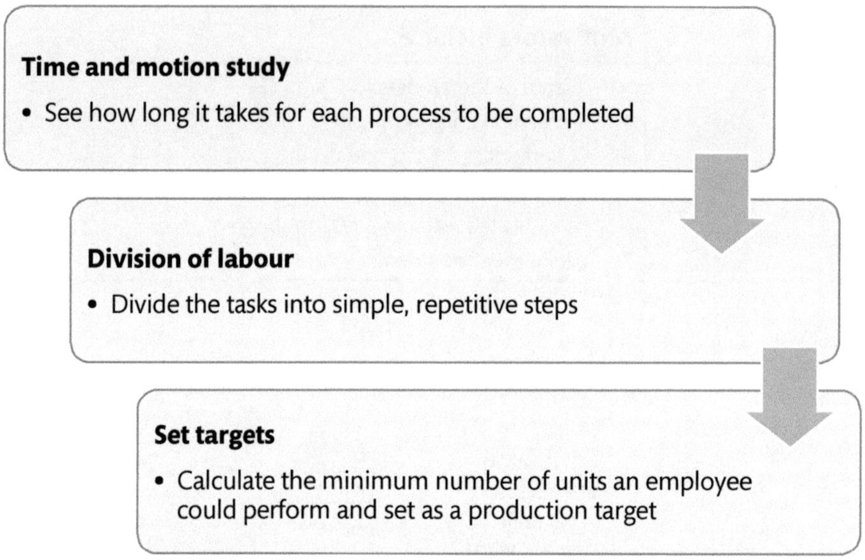

Time and motion study
• See how long it takes for each process to be completed
Division of labour
• Divide the tasks into simple, repetitive steps
Set targets
• Calculate the minimum number of units an employee could perform and set as a production target

Figure 2.3 *Taylor's scientific management approach prioritized productivity over employee motivation*

Exam tip

Many students state that **production-related pay** is bad for business as it costs a lot if employees produce large amounts. This is untrue, because as more product is made, more profit can be made.

Demotivated, bored staff
Disadvantages of Taylor's theory
Difficult to measure individual output
Prioritizes quantity over quality

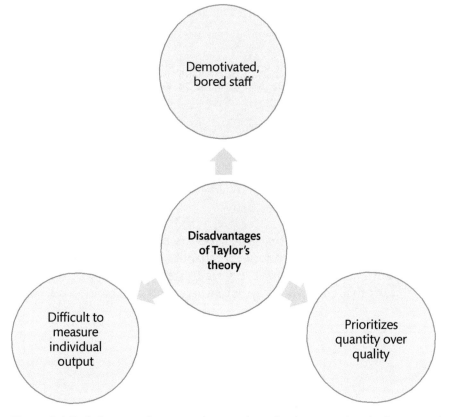

Figure 2.4 *Taylor's approach may produce results in the short term, but the long-term benefits of a motivated workforce are harder to achieve*

Herzberg's two-factor theory

Herzberg studied a smaller number of specific employees in the 1960s. He identified two different sets of needs that need to be met if employees are to be motivated.

Hygiene factors include:	Motivators include:
▶ job security	▶ a sense of achievement
▶ job status	▶ recognition for good work
▶ wages, salaries and other rewards	▶ opportunities for promotion
▶ working conditions and environment	▶ interesting and varied work
▶ relationships with managers	▶ being trusted with more responsibility
▶ rules and regulations in the organization.	▶ personal development.

Figure 2.5 *Herzberg's two-factor theory*

Exam tip

According to Herzberg, an employee cannot be easily motivated if hygiene factors are not met.

If an employee only has one set of needs met, (hygiene or motivators) then the employee will not be satisfied and the business will not have the benefit of a well-motivated workforce.

 Worked example

Identify and explain two disadvantages of using Taylors theory of scientific management. (4)

One disadvantage is that employees are paid by output. This means that they might focus on quantity over quality. Another disadvantage is that employees are treated like machines. This means that employees may not be very motivated.

2.1.3 Methods of motivation

As mentioned on page 33, methods of motivation can be separated into financial and non-financial.

Financial rewards

Labour is paid for in a variety of ways depending on the type of labour done, the employee being paid and the performance of the employee.

Permanent staff and managers are often paid a salary, which is an annual figure divided into 12 and paid monthly in return for an agreed number of hours worked per week. Payment amounts do not change unless the contract changes.

Temporary staff and employees working in retail, catering and mass production are often paid a wage. This can be paid as a:

- **time rate** – according to the number of hours worked
- **piece rate** – according to the number of units of output produced.

Performance-related pay is paid on reaching targets or goals. Forms of performance-related pay include:

- commission – based on number of sales
- bonus payments – one-off payments made for reaching specific targets
- profit share – a percentage of total profits paid to every employee
- share ownership – awarding part ownership of the business, allowing for dividend payments.

Non-financial rewards

Non-financial rewards are any rewards that cannot be turned into a cash payment. They should not be confused with pay or benefits, although they are often privileges afforded to employees who have performed well.

Reward	Explanation
Job rotation	Employees are trained to complete more than one task, which reduces boredom and increases teamwork.
Job enrichment	Employees' responsibilities are increased without additional reward, but with the provision of training.
Teamworking	Teams are created to encourage cooperation and feelings of control and ownership.
Training	Workers' skills are improved or expanded, meaning the employee may be eligible for promotion.
Promotion opportunities	Employees are provided with the chance to move up within the firm.

Exam tip

Not all rewards work for all people or situations; effective rewards must be tailored to the needs of the recipient.

Review

Before you continue, make sure you are able to understand and explain:

- the importance and benefits of a well-motivated workforce
- how businesses motivate employees
- the theories of Maslow, Taylor and Herzberg.

You need to know:
- how to draw, interpret and understand simple organizational charts
- the role of management
- leadership styles
- about trade unions.

 Recap

Business have structures to organize themselves to meet objectives. Employees within the structure are allocated roles with a certain level of responsibility and authority.

2.2.1 Why do businesses have organizational structures?

The purpose of **organizational structures** is explained in Figure 2.6.

Figure 2.6 *All businesses must be able to define their organizational structures*

Exam tip

The organizational structure is a simple view of the chain of command.

What are the elements of an organizational structure

Organizational charts show how individuals and departments are organized in a clear and logical fashion.

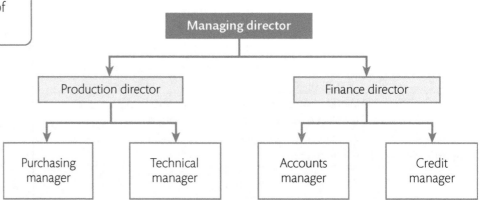

Figure 2.7 *The top three levels of an organizational structure might look like this*

To show the relationships between different levels of management and employees, there is specific terminology that must be used.

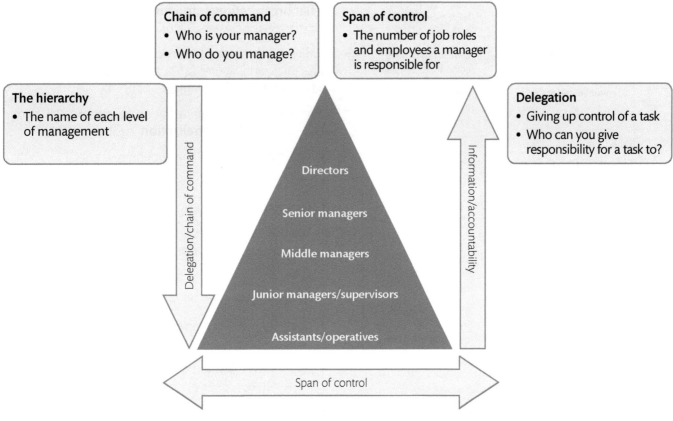

Figure 2.8 The terminology used in organizational structures helps stakeholders to understand their roles and responsibilities, as well as who is in charge of them and who they are in charge of

There are some key reasons for a clear **chain of command**. The higher up the pyramid a manager is, the more responsibility the manager has.

A clear chain of command is important to ensure:

- key business decisions and actions agreed by senior management are communicated effectively through the different levels

- responsibility and accountability is delegated at the appropriate level

- decision-making information can be passed up the chain of command to help make decisions.

Tall and flat hierarchical structures

There are two main types of hierarchical structure; tall and flat.

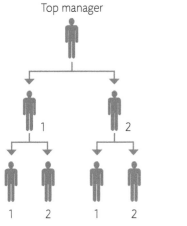

Figure 2.9a A tall management structure

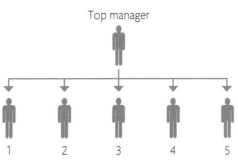

Figure 2.9b A flat organizational structure

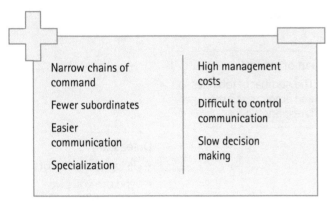

Figure 2.10a *Tall management structure*

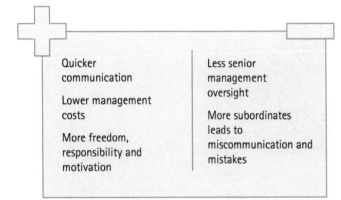

Figure 2.10b *Flat management structure*

A **tall management structure** is when there are many layers of management and a long chain of command.

A **flat organizational structure** is when there are almost no managers between executives and employees.

Figure 2.9 shows the differences between these two structures, and Figures 2.10a and 2.10b shows the advantages and disadvantages of both.

Another way of describing flat structures is to call them decentralized. **Decentralization** involves:

- reducing levels of management
- increasing the speed of decision making
- increasing the responsibility of junior managers
- keeping strategic decision-making responsibility but delegating tactical decision making.

This leads to:

- businesses being more responsive to market changes
- ideas from junior managers with current experience being utilized
- local knowledge and market conditions being considered
- increased creativity.

Exam tip

Tall structures are usually associated with established businesses, while flat structures are more associated with younger businesses.

Worked example

What is meant by a 'hierarchical structure'? (2)

A hierarchical structure is a visual representation of the levels of management in a business that shows the areas of a manager's responsibility.

Roles and responsibilities through the levels of hierarchy

Level	Overall responsibility	Detail
Directors or owners	Running the business	Usually responsible for a specific department within the organizational structure. Responsibilities include: • developing and setting long-term business objectives • monitoring and controlling departmental activities in relation to business objectives.
Managers	Responsible for specific areas within a department	Usually supervise activities, managers and/or other resources. Levels of management include senior, middle and junior. Responsibilities include: • carrying out long-term business objectives by setting specific targets for junior staff • motivating staff and monitoring employees' performance, identifying training needs and controlling budgets.

Level	Overall responsibility	Detail
Supervisors	Responsible for specific activities within an area	Usually supervise employees. Often recruited from within and promoted for initiative and leadership qualities.
		Responsibilities include: • closely managing daily output and targets • solving routine problems and resolving disputes.

2.2.2 The role of management

Management is the process of achieving business objectives through the best use of **resources**, including people.

The functions of management

Planning →
- Setting aims and objectives for an organization or area
- Creating business strategies and actions to meet these aims
- Providing training to ensure employees have the necessary skills to fulfill business objectives

Organizing →
- Managing employees and other resources
- Identifying roles, skills and resources required
- Making sure resources are available in good time

Coordinating →
- Bringing together all resources to achieve objectives
- Ensuring all departments and teams work together
- Managing problems and overcoming obstacles

Commanding →
- Giving instructions to employees
- Having authority to make decisions
- Guiding and motivating employees

Controlling →
- Measuring and assessing performance against objectives
- Putting corrective actions in place if targets not met
- Disciplining and imposing sanctions on employees who do not meet organizational requirements

> **Exam tip**
>
> Managers may be called by different names such as directors, supervisors or team leaders. However, they all manage resources.

> **Worked example**
>
> Identify and explain two functions of a manager. (6)
>
> > One function of a manager is to plan the raw materials of a business to make sure they don't run out. Another function is to organize the labour to make sure that there are enough employees available to meet production targets.

Skills and qualities of a good manager

There are many ways to describe a good manager. Some of the main skills and qualities a good manager must have are shown in Figure 2.11.

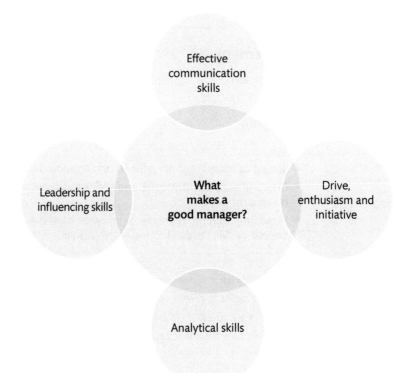

Figure 2.11 *Good management is crucial to the success of a workforce*

The importance of delegation

A good manager must also be able to **delegate** responsibility to junior managers. As businesses grow, the owner may have to allow others to make decisions.

Business organization	Who owns the business?	Who controls the business?
Sole trader	A single owner	The owner
Partnership	Partners	Senior partners have more control than other partners
Limited company	Shareholders	The board of directors and senior managers
Franchise	The franchisee	The franchisor controls many aspects of the business

As businesses grow:

- there are too many decisions to be made by one person
- the skills of the original owner may not be strong enough, and an expert can make better decisions
- hierarchies are created which show who is responsible for what.

What is needed for successful delegation?

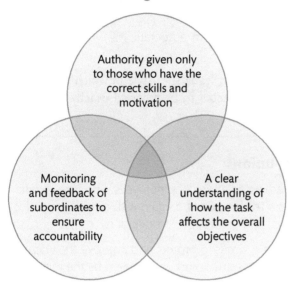

Authority given only to those who have the correct skills and motivation

Monitoring and feedback of subordinates to ensure accountability

A clear understanding of how the task affects the overall objectives

Figure 2.12 *Delegation is the reassignment of tasks by a superior to a subordinate employee or group of employees*

Exam tip

Delegation means giving a junior member authority to complete a task, but does not always take the responsibility for the task away from a manager (see Figure 2.12).

2.2.3 Leadership styles

When a manager leads employees, the manager has to have an effective style of leadership. Factors that affect leadership styles include:

- personality
- personal and business objectives
- the amount of authority
- the task.

There are three main styles of leadership **autocratic**, **democratic** and **laissez-faire**. They are shown in the table below.

Leadership styles		
Autocratic	*Democratic*	*Laissez-faire*
Gives clear and specific instructions	Employees are consulted and involved in decision making	Managers communicate objectives but then allow subordinates to organize own work to achieve objectives
No debate or discussion	Two-way communication with discussion of ideas	Encourages employee creativity and decision making
No chance for employees to challenge ideas	Ensures employee participation and satisfaction	Good for creative employees where deadlines are not important
Good for emergencies or when time is a factor	Can slow down decision making and action	Can cause confusion and inaction due to a lack of leadership
Can cause employee dissatisfaction		

Figure 2.13a *Autocratic management*

Figure 2.13b *Democratic management*

Worked example

What is meant by the term 'autocratic'? (2)

> Autocratic means a leadership style in which clear instructions are given and expected to be followed exactly as told.

2.2.4 Trade unions

Trade unions are associations of employees who have similar job roles within business. **Trade unions** bargain with employers collectively. The more members a union has, the stronger it is.

Trade unions' main aim is to protect and improve the wages and welfare of member employees. This can be achieved by the functions shown in Figure 2.14.

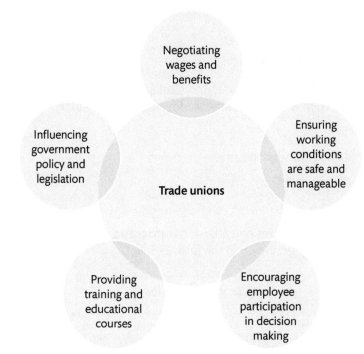

Figure 2.14 *Trade unions represent employees, and can be influential in private and public sector organizations, as well as on governments and political parties*

Trade unions can influence business decisions by disrupting business activity. This happens when all members agreeing to support a particular form of **industrial action**.

Forms of industrial action	
Overtime ban	Workers refuse to work more than their normal hours.
Work to rule	Workers deliberately slow down production by complying rigidly with every rule and regulation.
Go-slow	Work is carried out deliberately slowly to reduce production.
Strike	Workers refuse to work and may also protest, or **picket** outside their workplace to stop deliveries and prevent non-unionized workers from entering.

Worked example

Identify and explain one advantage and one disadvantage to a business of having a trade union. (4)

One advantage is that the employees will be motivated because their concerns about *[use example in the text]* will be listened to and important. One disadvantage is that the trade unions may stop production if the concerns about *[use example in the text]* are not met.

There are a number of effects of industrial action:

Effects of industrial action	
On business	Loss of output
	Loss of profits
	May lead to loss of customers to rivals
On employees	Loss of income
	May lose jobs if business is forced to **downsize** or close
On customers	Cannot obtain goods and services on time
	May have to pay higher prices to cover increased costs
On the economy	Frequent strike action may deter investors
	Revenue decreases
	May affect ability to pay for state services

⏱ **Review**

Before you continue, make sure you are able to:

- draw, interpret and understand simple organizational charts

- understand and explain hierarchical structures, including their terminology

- understand and explain the roles and responsibilities between different levels of hierarchy

- understand and explain the role and functions of management, including the importance of delegation

- explain different leadership styles

- recommend and justify appropriate leadership styles in different circumstances

- describe and explain the concept of trade unions and the benefits of membership.

Exam tip

Industrial disputes can be solved by **arbitration**, a process in which independent referee negotiates a compromise.

You need to know:
- how to recruit and select employees
- the importance and methods of training
- why workforce reduction may be necessary
- employment law and its effects on employees and employers.

Exam tip

Students often fail to clearly show the difference between recruitment (which is attracting employees) and selection (which is choosing the most suitable candidate).

2.3.1 The main stages of recruitment and selection

Recruitment and **selection** involve attracting and choosing the most suitable employee for the organization.

Worked example

What is meant by 'selection'? (2)

> Selection means to choose the most appropriate candidate based on the details of the job analysis.

Identify the job vacancy

What does the job entail (job analysis)? Write a job description

What type of person is needed to fill the job? Write a person specification

Advertise the job and send out details and application forms on request

Compare job applications with the person specification to select a shortlist of the best applicants to interview

Send invitations to attend interviews to job applicants who were shortlisted

If the applicant is not shortlisted, send a letter of regret

Prepare and conduct job interviews

Select the best applicant and make a formal job offer in writing

Draw up a contract of employment

Figure 2.15 *The stages involved in recruitment and selection*

Recruitment

Before you can select an appropriate employee you must first create a pool of talent by attracting **applicants** to apply for the position.

Advantages of internal recruitment	Disadvantages of internal recruitment
✓ It can save time and money over external recruitment.	✖ It creates other vacancies elsewhere in the organization.
✓ It allows the business to reward and retain high-performing employees.	✖ It prevents recruiting people with new ideas and skills into the business from other organizations that may have more efficient methods.
✓ Existing employees already know the business and working practices.	
✓ Opportunities for new jobs and promotions help motivate employees.	✖ It may create jealousy among competing employees for the job vacancy.

How can businesses attract potential employees

Businesses need to advertise their **vacancies** to attract potential employees to apply for the jobs. Often, the more people that apply, the better chance the business has of selecting the best candidate.

Different types of positions need different advertising methods, as different candidates look in different places for jobs. Some of the main methods are shown in Figure 2.16.

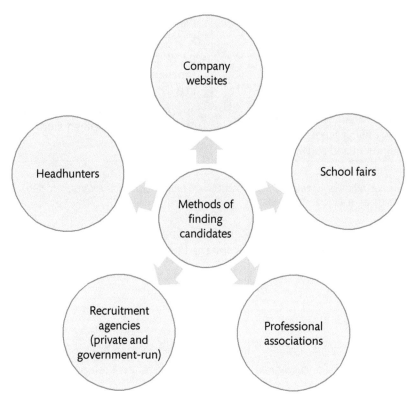

Figure 2.16 *Finding the right candidate for a role is about knowing where to look*

Selection

Once a business has advertised a vacant position, candidates apply for the job. There are three main ways in which an applicant can show a potential employer their skills and experience:

1. Using an **application form**
2. By submitting a **CV** or **résumé**
3. By writing an **application letter**.

Application form*	CV*	Letter of application*
An application form will normally require some or all of the following information to be provided by a job applicant: • personal details including name, address, telephone numbers, email address, date of birth, nationality • title of job applied for • schools, colleges and universities attended with dates • educational qualifications, for example, examination grades and dates taken • work experience, including previous jobs, former employers, main tasks and responsibilities • interests and hobbies • names and addresses of referees who can provide a reference (that is, give their opinion on the character and suitability of the applicant for the job).	A CV should be no more than one or two pages in length and will contain very similar information to an application form: • personal details including name, address, telephone numbers, email address, date of birth, nationality • schools, colleges and universities attended with dates • educational qualifications, examination grades and dates taken • work experience, including previous jobs, former employers, main tasks and responsibilities • names and addresses of referees to provide personal and employment references if required • interests and hobbies • any other relevant experience, for example, the ability to speak a foreign language, possession of a clean driving licence, ability to use IT equipment and software packages.	Sometimes applicants will be asked to write and submit a letter of application containing all the same information as an application form or CV would. However, more usually an applicant will send a short covering letter to accompany a CV. Writing a letter of application often requires more skills than completing an application form or CV. A human resources department will look for letters which are well written and presented and contain: • reasons for applying for the job • the skills, experience and qualities the applicant has and why he or she is well suited to the advertised job • details of relevant work and other experience if not already provided in a CV • any dates the applicant could not attend an interview if required.

* This symbol indicates sections of material that have been included as extension material, to put your studies in a broader context.

> **Exam tip**
>
> **Shortlisting** is matching the information given on a CV or résumé to the **job description** and **person specification**. This does not always mean the best candidates are selected.

Once the candidates have applied, the HR department must select the best candidates to **interview** by shortlisting the best candidates on paper.

Once shortlisted, the candidate is then invited to an interview. The main purpose of interviews is to:

• confirm factual information

• assess communication and interpersonal skills

• identify strengths and weaknesses that are not clear on the application form

• assess whether the person will fit into the organization

• select the most suitable candidate.

Full-time and part-time employees

Potential employees can be offered full- or part-time employment. Each country has different general expectations of full-time employment.

Full-time employment has the following benefits and limitations:

Benefits to employers	Benefits to employees
✓ Full-time employees work fixed, predictable hours. ✓ Full-time employees are more likely to develop loyalty and be more committed to their employer. ✓ The employees usually only hold one job, making it easier to control their time and productive efforts. ✓ They can continue to run a business in the owner's or senior manager's absence.	✓ Full-time employees have fixed, predictable hours of employment. ✓ Wages per hour are usually higher than those paid to part-time employees doing the same or similar jobs. ✓ Annual leave, sick leave, health insurance and other benefits may be more generous than those offered to part-time employees. ✓ Full-time jobs are often considered to be part of a career, with more chance of receiving training and promotions to reach more senior positions.
Limitations to employers	**Limitations to employees**
✗ Full-time employees may not want to work extended hours. ✗ Those who agree to work evenings and weekends will have to be paid premium or overtime wage rates. ✗ Annual leave and other benefits given to full-time employees are costly.	✗ Less time is available for leisure activities or spending with family and friends. ✗ Full-time employees may be required to work overtime on top of normal hours. ✗ The work may be boring and lack variety.

Figure 2.17a *Benefits and limitations of full-time employment*

Part-time employment has the following benefits and limitations:

Benefits to employers	Benefits to employees
✓ Part-time employees can be an excellent staffing option for new and small businesses, due to the flexibility they offer and their relatively low cost. ✓ A business can vary the number of hours each part-time employee works based on the amount of work available, for example, requiring them to work more hours at busy times. ✓ Part-time employees may not qualify for all the same benefits as full-time employees and are therefore cheaper to employ.	✓ Part-time employment offers people more flexibility, for example, to look after family members, continue in education or pursue their other interests. ✓ Some part-time employees may have more than one job, providing them with more variety in their work and teaching them more skills. ✓ There may be more and a greater variety of part-time jobs open to an employee than full-time employment opportunities.
Limitations to employers	**Limitations to employees**
✗ Some part-time employees may hold more than one job which may make them less loyal to their employer than full-time employees. ✗ Turnover is often higher. This means recruitment and selection costs may be higher because part-time employees tend to change their jobs more often than full-time employees. ✗ Part-time employees may not be as skilled or as productive as full-time employees and may require more training. ✗ It can be difficult to communicate with part-time employees during periods when they are not in work. For example, they may miss important business meetings.	✗ The wages rates may be lower than that in an equivalent or similar full-time job. These employees may have to take another part-time job to boost their earnings. ✗ They may not qualify for the same benefits full-time employees receive from their employers, such as health insurance. ✗ They may receive less training than full-time employees because their employers think they are less likely to stay with them in the same job for as long or want promotion. ✗ They may be less likely to be promoted to more senior positions because they do not work full-time. ✗ They may miss important business meetings.

Figure 2.17b *Benefits and limitations of part-time employment*

2.3.2 Training

The importance of training

Employees can be viewed as one of the most important resources of a business. **Training** can be important for both the business and the employee. The advantages for employers include:

- reduced supervision costs
- reduced number of accidents
- multi-skilled and adaptable workforces
- objectives are more easily met.

For employees, the advantages include:

- increased job satisfaction and motivation
- promotions and salary increases
- help to remain engaged and focused.

Methods of training

Induction

- provided to new employees
- helps to adjust to organization and work environment
- general information such as health and safety, facilities and contacts

On-the-job (shadowing)

- usually for unskilled or semi-skilled employees
- employee works with a mentor who trains while working
- specific to the task and role – applied learning

Off-the-job training

- employees attend training and education away from their place of work
- classes taught by experts – theoretical learning

 Worked example

Identify and explain two disadvantages of 'on-the-job training'. (4)

One disadvantage is that if the person doing the training has bad habits, the person being trained will learn these habits. Another disadvantage is that the employee does not get a certificate, which means that the person has no proof of being trained if applying for another job.

> **Exam tip**
>
> Even though training can be expensive and may at first seem to reduce profits, trained employees increase productivity, efficiency and overall profitability.

2.3.3 Workforce reduction

When businesses plan their workforce needs, they sometimes need to reduce as well as increase the **workforce**. There are several methods a business can use to reduce a workforce:

1. Not replacing employees who leave or retire.

2. Making employees redundant when their job role is no longer necessary.

3. Dismissing employees because rules have been broken.

The difference between redundancy and dismissal

When a business actively chooses to reduce the workforce (instead of relying on employees to leave by themselves), it is either through **redundancy** or **dismissal** (see Figure 2.18).

Redundancy
- Occurs when the organization no longer needs the skills of an employee
- The employee's performance is not relevant
- Employees receive compensation for losing their job

Dismissal
- The employee's performance or behaviour does not meet organizational requirements leading to the termination of the employee's contract
- There are several stages of the disciplinary procedure that are usually followed, including verbal and written warnings
- No compensation is provided

Figure 2.18 Employees can be subject to redundancy or dismissal at any time

The reasons a business may downsize

Reasons a business may downsize	
Labour substitution	New technologies and equipment
	More cost effective
Lack of demand	Increased competition
	Changing consumer tastes
Closure of business premises	Relocation overseas
	Change in distribution methods
	Business failure
Integration	Mergers or takeovers reduce number of employees required
	Non-core areas closed
	Redundancies

Exam tip

Workforce planning involves a business changing the size and composition of its workforce to meet current and future needs based on aims, objectives and targets.

Worked example

What is meant by the term 'downsizing'? (2)

> Downsizing means to reduce the size of a business's workforce to meet future needs.

2.3.4 Employment law

Different countries have different legal controls over employment issues. However, these legal controls have different impacts on both employees and employers. Most **employment law** includes the rights to:

- a written statement of terms and conditions
- protection from unfair dismissal and **discrimination**
- a safe and healthy environment
- wage protection (such as a minimum wage).

Employment contracts

These are used to regulate the relationship between employers and employees and ensure that both parties understand what is expected from a contract of employment.

There are three main types of employment contracts:

1. **Permanent full-time contracts**
    - 35 hours per week or more
    - No end date

2. **Permanent part-time contracts**
    - Fewer than 35 hours per week
    - No end date

3. **Fixed-term contracts**
    - Can be full or part-time
    - Covers a specific time period

Employment contracts will often include details of:

- wage rate or salary
- frequency of payments
- salary or wage review dates
- expectations and responsibilities.

Effects on employees	Effects on employers
Certainty of wages and safety of employment	Allows employers to direct employees to carry out specific tasks
Clarifies employer expectations	Allows employers to discipline employees for gross misconduct or incompetence
Can be used as a way of challenging bullying or discrimination	Prevents employers from instructing employees to carry out tasks outside of their contracts

Unfair dismissal

Employees can take their employers to an employment tribunal if they feel that they have been **unfairly dismissed**.

Examples of reasons for unfair dismissal:

- differences in race, religion sex or disability

- pregnancy

- illness

- joining a trade union.

Unfair dismissal protection, which forms part of employment law, affects employees and employers, as shown in the table below.

Effects on employees	Effects on employers
Ensures employees cannot be dismissed for no reason	Means employers cannot dismiss employees without reason
Provides compensation	Increases regulatory costs

Discrimination

Most countries try to ensure unfair **discrimination** is illegal.

There are three types of unfair discrimination:

1. **Direct discrimination**: to be obviously treated less favourably due to any differences

2. **Indirect discrimination:** to be discriminated against due to an inability to meet an unjustified requirement.

3. **Victimization:** to be discriminated against repeatedly for one or many reasons.

Discrimination protection forms a part of employment law, and its effects are shown in the table below.

Effects on employees	Effects on employers
Provides safe working environment	Ensures happy workforce
Creates equal working environment	Reduces negative publicity

> **Exam tip**
>
> It is legal to discriminate on experience, performance and ability because these are measureable elements which affect the ability to fulfill a job role. It is illegal to discriminate on gender, race, age, disability or pregnancy.

Worked example

> What is meant by 'unfair discrimination'? (2)
>
> > Discrimination means to be treated less favourably than other people based on factors such as race or sex.

Health and safety

There are laws to protect employees from danger at work. Examples of **health and safety** laws include:

- minimum working conditions, including working hours

- protective equipment supplied for hazardous roles

- training and inspections.

The table below shows the effects of health and safety laws.

Effects on employees	Effects on employers
Reduces risk of injury and death	Reduces time and money lost due to stopped production
Improves working conditions	Increases employee motivation
Motivates employees to remain within business	Increases costs of safety equipment and training

Legal minimum wage

Many countries set a **minimum wage** that must be paid to employees to stop exploitation of the workforce.

It is illegal to make wage deductions unless it is a statutory requirement by law or is voluntary and agreed with the employee.

Wage protection forms a part of employment law, and its effects on employers and employees are shown in the table below.

Effects on employees	Effects on employers
Raises pay levels to minimum living levels	Increases wage costs
Protects vulnerable workers from pay discrimination	Reduces number of employees
Increases workload to meet productivity and profitability targets	May cause demands for price increases among higher-paid staff
	Raises prices of finished goods to cover increased costs

> **Exam tip**
>
> Legal controls are different all over the world and some businesses relocate to get the most cost-efficient workforce with the least control.

Review

Before you continue, make sure you are able to:

- define and explain the different elements of recruitment and selection
- explain the difference between internal and external recruitment
- list the benefits and limitations of part- and full-time staff
- identify and explain different training methods and their importance for employers and employees
- identify and explain the benefits and limitations of different types of training
- understand why reducing through redundancy or dismissal a workforce may be necessary
- understand why workforce reduction may be necessary
- identify and explain the legal controls over employment issues and their impact on employers and employees.

You need to know:
- the importance of different types of workplace communication
- different methods of communication in business
- the barriers to good business communication.

2.4.1 Communication

What is effective communication?

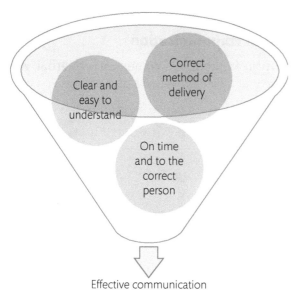

Effective communication

Figure 2.19 *A successful business must think carefully about how and when to communicate important messages*

> **Exam tip**
>
> It is important to understand that **communication** is a two-way process – the information must be given in a clear and correct manner but it must also be received by the recipient.

Worked example

What is effective communication? (2)

Effective communication is when a message is clear and easy to understand and is aimed at the correct person.

Why is effective communication important?

Without effective communication, business will not be able to achieve its aims and objectives. Communication must reach the recipient in a way that ensures that the message is understood. It is important to choose the correct medium for transmitting information.

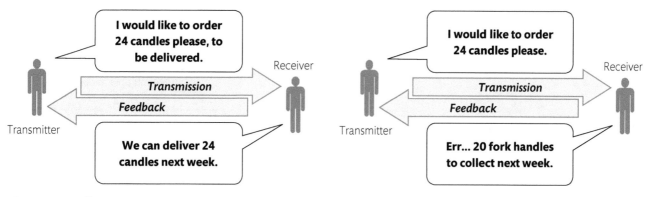

Figure 2.20a *Effective communications*

Figure 2.20b *Ineffective communications*

Exam tip

Businesses need to communicate effectively with both internal and external recipients.

Communications with customers	Communications with employees	Communications with other organizations
To sell goods and services through advertising and product information	To relay instructions and meet aims and objectives	To build relationships and contracts with suppliers, financial and governmental organizations
Receive orders, sales, enquires and complaints	Can be horizontal or vertical, and two-way or one-way	Ensure accurate records, payment and deliveries

Exam tip

Electronic communications are not considered a method; they are considered a means of communication, as verbal, written and visual communication can be either electronic or not.

2.4.2 Methods of communication

There are three main methods of communication: **verbal**, **written** and **visual**. Each have their advantages and disadvantages.

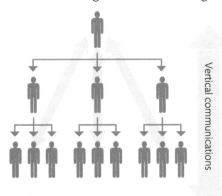

Verbal communication

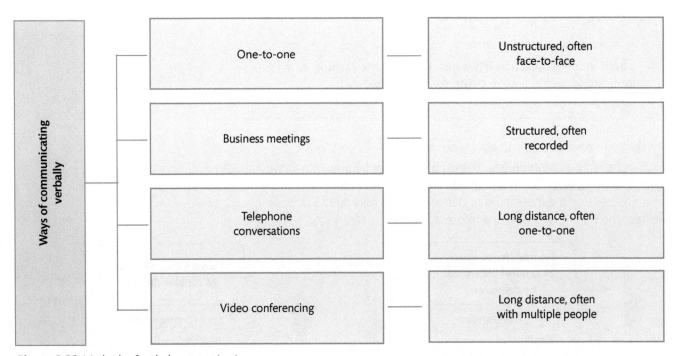

Figure 2.21 *Methods of verbal communication*

Advantages of verbal communications	Disadvantages of verbal communications
✓ Information and messages can be communicated instantly and to many people at the same time if business meetings are used. ✓ Messages in face-to-face meetings can be reinforced using facial expressions and body language. ✓ Written and visual materials can also be used to reinforce spoken messages. ✓ Feedback from the receiver or receivers can be immediate.	✗ It can be difficult to determine whether receivers are listening and understanding messages or information transmitted, especially on a telephone or in a big business meeting. ✗ Internet speeds and telephone line quality can vary. This can make telephone calls and videoconferencing difficult. ✗ Verbal communications rely on the sender and receiver being able to speak the same language well enough to understand each other. ✗ Verbal communications do not provide a record of discussions for later reference.

Written communication

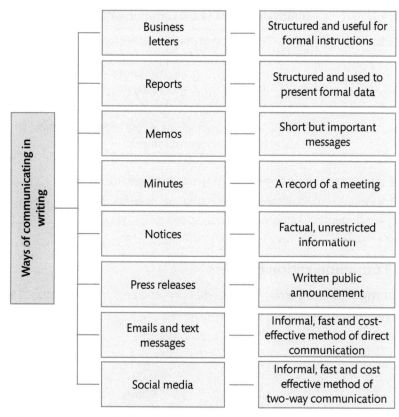

Figure 2.22 *Methods of written communication*

Advantages of written communications	Disadvantages of written communications
✓ One good thing about written communications is that they provide a record of messages and information sent and received. They can be referred to again at a later date if disagreements arise between a sender and receiver over the content of communications. ✓ They are useful for detailing long and complicated messages and information, such as instructions for operating machinery and equipment, and for laws and regulations. ✓ Written communications can be stored in filing cabinets or electronically and also copied for sending on to other receivers. ✓ Sending written communications using email and the internet is fast and cheap.	✗ It may be difficult to determine whether receivers have understood the messages or information transmitted in written communications. ✗ Some readers may have difficulty with technical terms and language used by some senders in their written communications. ✗ Immediate and direct feedback may not be possible unless the communications between the sender and receiver are electronic. ✗ Restricted written communications may "leak". This means they may be received by others, such as rival firms or the press, who are not supposed to receive them. This is because written communications can be copied.

Visual communication

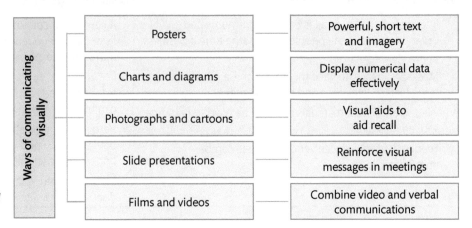

Figure 2.23 *Methods of visual communication*

Advantages of visual communications	Disadvantages of visual communications
✓ They can be used to illustrate or reinforce points made in verbal and written communications. ✓ They are an attractive and sometimes more interesting way of presenting information to a large number of receivers.	✗ It is difficult to determine whether receivers have understood the messages or information transmitted. ✗ Charts and diagrams may be difficult for some people to understand, especially if they contain financial and technical information. ✗ Some visual communications are expensive to produce, such as television advertisements.

Considerations when choosing methods of communication

It is important to understand not only the needs of the audience when choosing a method, but also the cost, speed of delivery and size of the audience.

2.4.3 Communication barriers

A **communication barrier** occurs when a message is misunderstood, does not target the right audience or is ineffective.

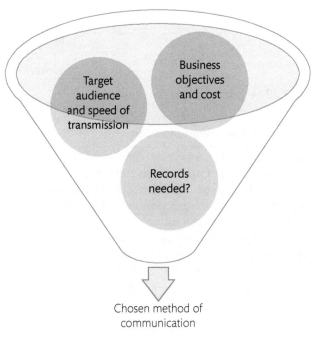

Figure 2.24 *Several factors influence an organization's choice of communication method*

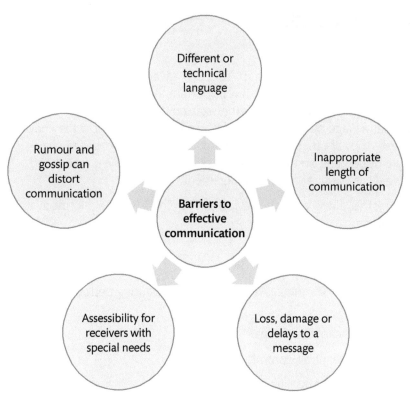

Figure 2.25 *Misunderstood, ineffective, or unreceived communications can be very costly to a business*

Communication barriers can be removed or minimized by:

- effective training
- short, clear and understandable messages
- understanding the target audience and its requirements.

Worked example

What is meant by 'a barrier to communication'? (2)

> A barrier to communication is something that makes a message to be misunderstood or not received, such as too much technical language.

Exam tip

It will never be possible to remove all communications barriers, as people will always miscommunicate.

Review

Before you continue, make sure you are able to:

- understand the importance of effective communication and the limitations and benefits of different methods
- demonstrate an awareness of communication barriers and how they can be reduced.

Exam-style questions

Unit 2

Frank and Ben are in a partnership. They sell advertising space in magazines to local businesses in country X. It is important that Frank and Ben have well-motivated employees. When they started their business they paid themselves a wage on the number of hours they worked. Now they have employees they are thinking of changing to a commission-based pay structure depending on the number of sales each employee makes and applying a laissez-faire style of management.

They think this, along with on-the-job sales training, will help to motivate the workforce.

(a) What is meant by 'motivation'? (2)

(b) Identify two advantages to Frank and Ben of using performance related pay. (2)

(c) What is meant by a 'wage'? (2)

(d) What is meant by 'commission'? (2)

(e) What is meant by 'laissez-faire'? (2)

(f) Identify and explain two disadvantages of using the laissez-faire style of management. (4)

(g) Identify two features of on-the-job sales training. (4)

(h) Identify and explain two benefits of on-the-job training in a sales environment. (6)

(i) Do you think Frank and Ben should change their payment method for sale of advertising space? Justify your answer. (6)

(j) Identify two methods of non-financial motivation Frank and Ben could use. (6)

Unit 3:
Marketing

Unit outline

As you have progressed through the concepts of **business activity** and **the people in business,** you will have discovered how businesses utilize resources in order to create goods and services to achieve business objectives.

This **marketing** chapter now will explore the various method businesses use to attract potential customers and the impacts of external factors on marketing decisions.

Your revision checklist

Either tick these boxes to build a record of your revision, *or* use them to identify your strengths and weaknesses.

Specification	Theme	☺	😐	☹
3.1 Marketing, competition and the customer	3.1.1 The role of marketing			
	3.1.2 How markets change			
	3.1.3 Niche and mass marketing			
	3.1.4 Market segmentation			
3.2 Market research	3.2.1 The roles, uses and methods of market research			
	3.2.2 Presenting and using market research results			
3.3 The marketing mix	3.3.1 What is the marketing mix?			
	3.3.2 Product			
	3.3.3 Price			
	3.3.4 Place			
	3.3.5 Promotion			
	3.3.6 Technology and the marketing mix			
3.4 Marketing strategy	3.4.1 Developing marketing strategies			
	3.4.2 Legal controls on marketing			
	3.4.3 Marketing in foreign markets			

You need to know:

- the role of marketing
- the causes and effects of market changes
- about concepts of niche marketing and mass marketing
- how and why market segmentation is undertaken.

 Recap

The role of **marketing** is to create the desire for a product or service by a supplier to entice a customer who is willing and able to buy the product. Marketing can be local, national or international, depending on the target audience.

Exam tip

A market is not always a physical place – it is any location where buyers and sellers meet.

3.1.1 The role of marketing

Marketing involves adapting the product, price and promotional strategy in response to changes in technology, policy, competition and consumer needs and wants.

What is the market?

A **market** is where all the consumers who are willing and able to buy a product or service can meet all the producers willing and able to supply the product or service. Examples of markets are shown in Figure 3.1.

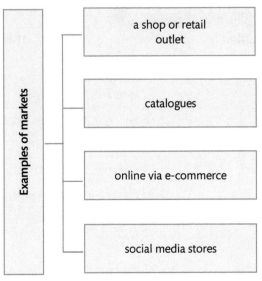

Figure 3.1 *A market doesn't have to be a physical location for buying and selling goods; increasingly markets are online*

Consumer needs and wants

Marketing includes the advertising and selling products and services in order to be successful. The points in Figure 3.2 must be considered.

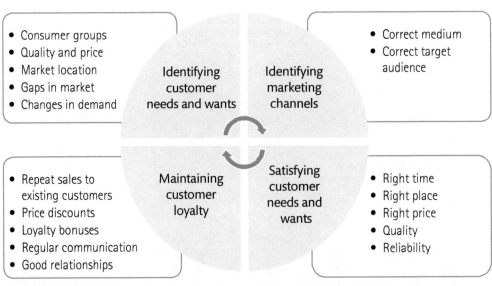

Figure 3.2 *Generating sales, satisfying customers and maintaining loyalty relies on a number of factors*

Building relationships

There are many reasons to build **relationships**, and many methods, as shown in Figure 3.3. Mostly, keeping existing customers is cheaper than attracting new custom from competitors.

How to build customer relationships	
Well-trained staff	Effective communications

Direct effect	
Great customer experience	Customer service

Impact on business	
Repeat custom	Prompt and efficient communication channels

Figure 3.3 Companies that build effective relationships with their customers will generate sales in both the short and the long term

Exam tip

Just because a product is expensive does not mean it is good quality – quality means the product does its intended function effectively.

Exam tip

It is important to understand and show your ability to link cause and effect.

Marketing objectives

It is important to understand what the objectives of the business are before deciding upon a **marketing strategy**. Most businesses will have a specific objective they wish to achieve. Some of these objectives are shown in Figure 3.4.

Figure 3.4 Effective marketing relies on clear objectives

Worked example

Identify and explain two possible marketing objectives for a business. (4)

> One marketing objective could be to raise consumer awareness. This will make more people aware of the brand.
> A second marketing objective could be to increase market share. This will increase the total number of customers buying the busines's products.

Recap

Markets are not static and change for many reasons. Some market conditions are predictable and can be planned for. Some changes however are unpredictable and businesses must be reactive.

3.1.2 How markets change

It is important to understand the market. To do this, we can ask the following questions:

- do markets change rapidly or slowly?
- what are the factors affecting change?
- how can the business react?

Market conditions can be the result of **demand-side** and **supply-side factors** (as shown in Figure 3.5).

Price factors

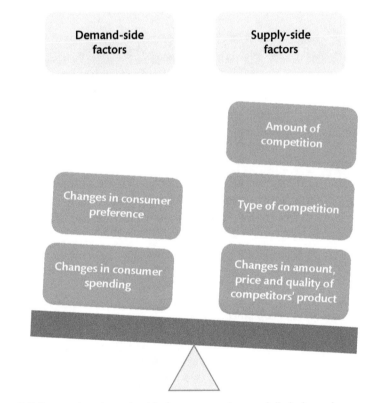

Figure 3.5 *Demand and supply-side factors must be carefully balanced*

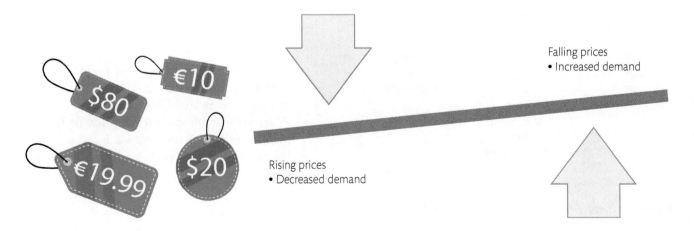

Figure 3.6 *The relationship between price and demand*

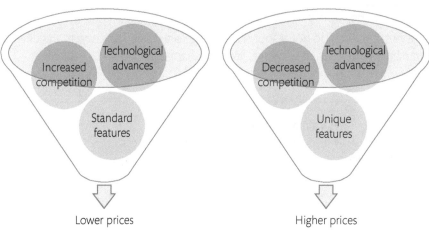

Figure 3.7 *Factors affecting price*

Worked example

What is meant by '**price competition**'? (2)

Price competition is rivalry between similar businesses using the selling price as the main feature.

Non-price factors

Markets are also influenced by **non-price factors**. The effects of these are shown in Figure 3.8.

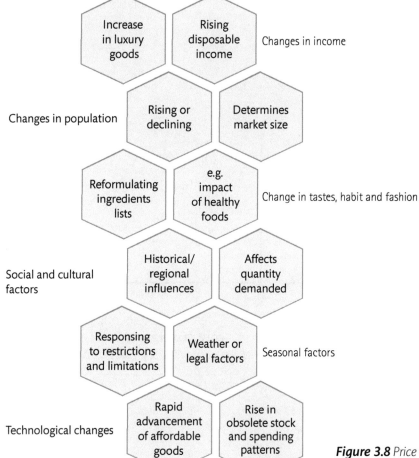

Figure 3.8 *Price is not the only consideration when making business decisions*

Business responses to change

Businesses which do not respond to change often fail. There are many different ways in which a business can respond to change, as shown in Figure 3.9.

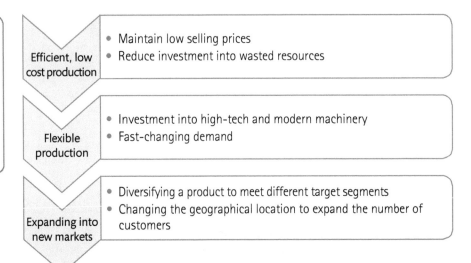

Figure 3.9 *Market conditions must be monitored carefully; and an organization's behaviour must be managed accordingly*

Businesses must be aware of whether a change is a short- or long-term trend.

Short-term fads or crazes may last a few hours, days or weeks and need instant response. Long-term trends may be observed by years and have steady and incremental alterations which are predictable and have a considered, measured response.

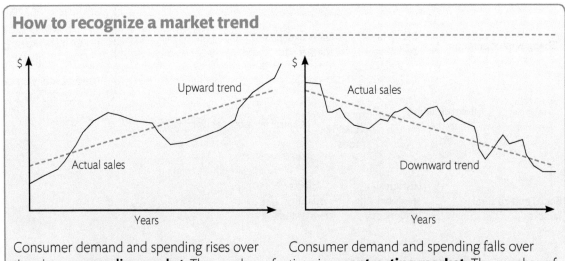

How to recognize a market trend

Consumer demand and spending rises over time in an **expanding market**. The number of producers supplying the market may also grow.

Consumer demand and spending falls over time in a **contracting market**. The number of producers supplying the market may also fall.

Why markets become competitive

As markets grow, **competition** increases. As more competitors enter the market, the same number of customers are divided between more suppliers. Therefore, competition increases for a number of reasons, as shown in Figure 3.10.

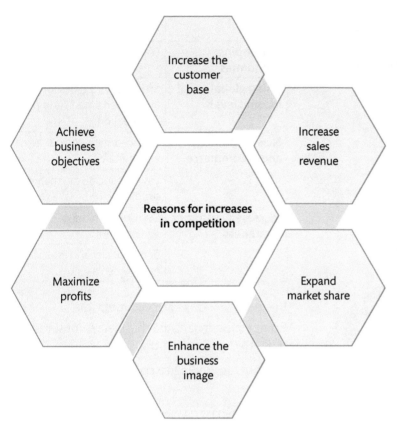

Figure 3.10 *Competition from other businesses affects decision making*

Businesses can compete on price and non-price factors (see Figure 3.11).

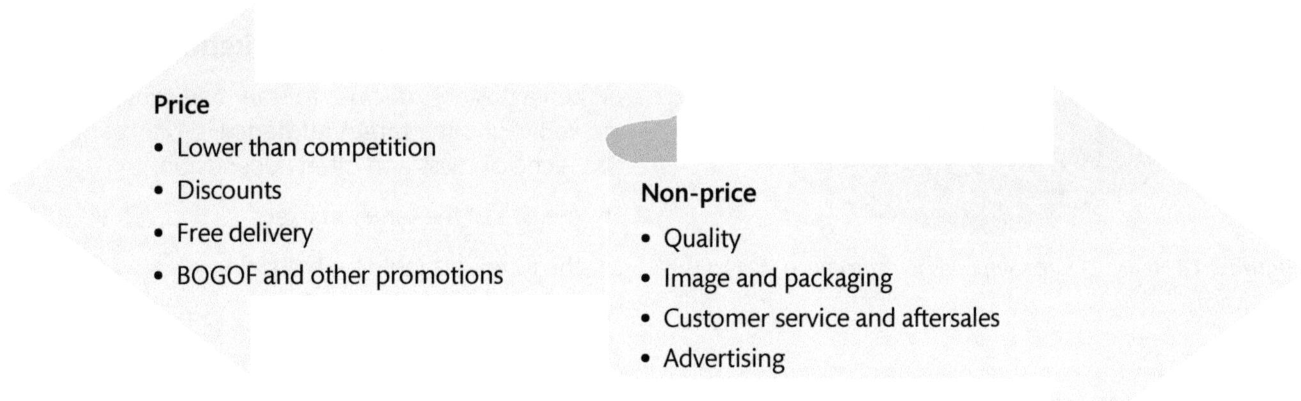

Price
- Lower than competition
- Discounts
- Free delivery
- BOGOF and other promotions

Non-price
- Quality
- Image and packaging
- Customer service and aftersales
- Advertising

Figure 3.11 *All the features of a product, and the services provided by the business, can be used to beat the competition*

Figure 3.12 *Some of the causes and effects of increased competition*

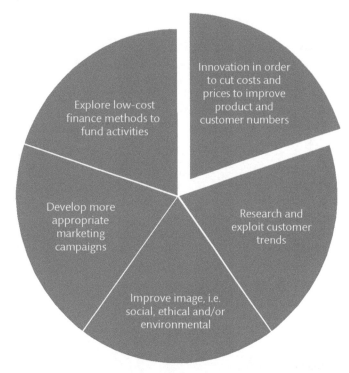

Figure 3.13 *How a business responds to competition is crucial to its survival*

When competition increases, there are a number of indicators that may be observed (see Figure 3.12).

Factors that increase competition in existing markets are listed and explained in the table below.

Factor	Reason
Developing economies	Lower production costs
Rising global income levels	More opportunities for international trade and overseas competition
New technology and e-commerce	Reduced start-up and capital expenditure
	Easier to locate alternative suppliers
Increased customer awareness	Demand for product information and best deals
	Better quality and ethical requirements

Business responses to competition

Competition means that businesses must respond in order to survive and grow.

Without responding to competition, businesses can lose:

- market share
- market power
- customer loyalty
- brand awareness.

3.1.3 Niche and mass marketing

When a business decides to start marketing, it needs to know who the **target audience** is. Marketing can be niche or mass and often depends on:

- the size of the target market
- the funds available for marketing
- customer expectations.

Mass marketing

Mass marketing does not target a specific group. This approach is usually used for the following types of goods and services:

- mass-produced
- homogenous
- low-priced.

Examples of **mass marketing** media include:

- national television
- national newspapers
- websites and social media.

The advantages and disadvantages of mass marketing are listed in the table below.

Advantages	Disadvantages
✓ Marketing economies of scale due to size of audience ✓ Ability to advertise several varieties of the same product at the same time	✗ High levels of competition ✗ Can still be expensive due to production and advertising costs ✗ May limit brand appeal due to mass image

Niche marketing

Niche marketing targets specific groups of customers who prefer specialized and exclusive products. These customers are often overlooked by mass producers or are thought of as unprofitable. Characteristics of niche market products are that they are:

- made-to-order/unique
- design, quality and reputation
- low-volume.

Examples of **niche marketing** media include:

- local newspapers or magazines
- blogs and speciality websites
- flyers and leaflets.

The advantages and disadvantages of niche marketing are listed in the table below.

Advantages	Disadvantages
✓ Less competition ✓ Lower costs as product quality is more important than advertising ✓ Attracts high-value customers ✓ Creates a reputation of specialism	✗ Limited opportunities for sales and growth ✗ Often relies on one customer segment, so a change in consumer buying habits may cause business failure

Worked example

Identify two possible benefits of niche marketing. (2)

> There is usually less competition. Customers are usually willing to pay a higher price.

Exam tip

Just because a business uses niche marketing does not mean the product is high value, exclusive or unique.

Recap

Market segmentation divides the whole market into smaller segments, each with similar features, such as:

- characteristics
- preferences
- buying habits.

Market segmentation should occur before the business designs its product and methods of promotion. Effective market segmentation should:

- identify a target market
- identify the wants and needs of the target market
- ensure that most appropriate features are promoted
- ensure that effective methods of promotion are used.

Exam tip

Markets can be segmented into large or small groups depending on whether mass or niche marketing is going to be used.

Exam tip

Be careful not to stereotype groups. For instance, not *all* men like football.

Worked example

What is meant by market segmentation? (2)

Market segmentation is dividing a whole market into different groups that each share similar characteristics.

3.1.4 Market segmentation

How to segment markets

There are many ways of segmenting markets, as shown in Figure 3.14.

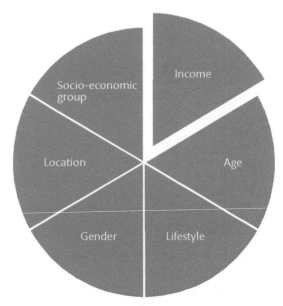

Figure 3.14 *Market segmentation*

Benefits of segmentation

If a business is able to segment the market effectively, there are a number of benefits that can be seen:

1. **More effective marketing** – appeals to the price, place, product and promotional preferences of the target customer.
2. **Easier to identify gaps in the market** – products can be adapted to exploit unmet needs.
3. **Increased sales and profits** – a larger customer base with specific needs leads to increased income.

Review

Before you continue, make sure you are able to:

- describe the role of marketing in identifying and satisfying customer needs
- explain the importance of maintaining customer loyalty and building relationships
- understand and explain market changes and business response
- understand and explain changing customer spending patterns and needs
- say why some markets become competitive and how businesses can respond
- describe and apply the concepts of niche and mass marketing
- understand and explain the reasons for and methods of market segmentation.

You need to know:
- the role of market research and methods used
- presentation and use of market research results.

3.2.1 The roles, uses and methods of market research

 Recap

Market research is a tool to gather data on:

- customer preferences
- spending patterns
- threats from rivals and substitutes
- changing market conditions.

There is a process that is followed when collecting market research, as shown in Figure 3.15.

Stage 1
What is the purpose of the market research? What information is needed? What action will be taken as a result of the research findings, for example, change product design or alter the pricing strategy.

↓

Stage 2
Decide on the most appropriate research methods, depending on the amount of time and budget available to spend.

↓

Stage 3
Design a questionnaire. Determine how consumers should be asked questions. Decide what characteristics (age, sex, income, lifestyle, etc.) those people asked should have. Identify secondary sources of relevant market research data.

↓

Stage 4
Undertake the research.

↓

Stage 5
Analyse the results, draw conclusions and produce a report of the findings. Make recommendations and decisions on the future marketing strategy.

Figure 3.15 *The stages of market research*

Uses of market research

The results of market research can be used by a market-oriented business to:

- reduce the risk of developing and producing unappealing products and services
- increase the ability to identify and target a specific market
- create an effective marketing mix
- increase sales and profits.

Exam tip

Marketing is not limited to methods of promotion – the marketing mix must be utilized by successful companies.

Market research information

Product

What products do consumers want?
What product features do they like most?
What is the consumer reaction to new products?

Price

How much are consumers willing to pay?
What methods do they prefer to use to make a payment?

Place and method of sale

Where do consumers prefer to shop?
What is the reaction of retailers to new products?
Are consumers satisfied with customer service?

Promotions

How effective have promotional campaigns been?
How do consumers react to different promotional ideas?

Market

What is the size of the market?
Is the market expanding or contracting?
What are the main characteristics (age, sex, lifestyle, etc.) of existing and potential customers?

Competition

Who are the main business competitors?
What are their strengths and weaknesses?
What are their market shares?
How do they promote their products?
What are their pricing strategies?

Types of market research

There are two types of **data** that can be gathered:

1. **Quantitative data**
   - easy to gather large amounts of data quickly
   - easy to count and analyse
   - can create effective visual graphs and charts
   - includes statistics such as price, quantity and market share.

2. **Qualitative data**
   - difficult to analyse large amounts of data
   - useful for providing reasons for quantitative data
   - includes opinions judgments or reactions, often verbal or written.

This data can be collected in two different ways, and from a number of different sources.

Methods of primary research

Primary data is new data collected by the business or on the business's behalf.

Primary data can be expensive to collect but has some advantages:

- it meets the specific requirements of the organization, so should be 100 per cent useful
- it is up to date and is better than previously published sources
- the data is exclusive.

Methods of collecting primary data are shown in Figure 3.16.

Interviews and surveys
- ✓ Cost-effective method of gathering quantitative and qualitative data
- ✓ Can target specific market segments
- ✗ Difficulty in encouraging participation – low response rates
- ✗ Time consuming to gather and analyse data
- ✗ Interviewer bias may be evident in the questions and methods of delivery

Focus groups
- ✓ Gathers a range of opinions in one time and place
- ✓ Creates discussion and different points of view from different participants
- ✗ Time consuming and expensive to set up
- ✗ Members may be influenced by other reactions and may not give true opinions

Observation and test marketing
- ✓ Cost effective in gaining large amounts of quantitative data
- ✓ Reduces the risk of promotional failure by testing small-scale consumer reactions
- ✗ Time consuming and often no qualitative reason for results
- ✗ Different groups in different regions may have different reactions so may be hard to extrapolate

Figure 3.16 *Primary data collection methods have advantages and disadvantages*

Sampling

To make sure a business gets a good range of results, it must create a **sampling** strategy. The most common methods are **random** and **quota** sampling.

Methods of secondary research

Secondary (or desk-based) research using existing sources is often used by businesses to gain market information. Data can be from internal or external sources.

Internal methods of secondary research are shown in Figure 3.17.

Figure 3.17 *Internal methods of secondary research*

External sources are shown in Figure 3.18.

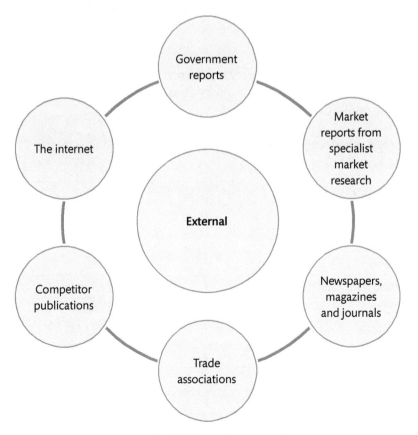

Figure 3.18 *External methods of secondary research*

The accuracy of market research data and influencing factors

There are many reasons for inaccurate primary data research. Some common faults are listed in the table below.

Sampling bias	The sample chosen may not be representative of the customer base.
Questionnaire bias	Misleading or badly worded questions influence answers.
Response bias	Some respondents may not give accurate answers due to many factors including image, politeness and misremembering data.
Poor questionnaire design	Questions may be too open-ended or guiding. Confusing questions may result in respondents giving any answer. Questions may force respondents into answering in the preferred fashion.
Poor use of open and closed questioning	Closed questions (limited to 'yes', 'no' or a specified answer) are useful for an initial factual answer, but should be followed by an open (opinion-based) answer to elaborate on the reason.
Not testing the questionnaire	It is important to identify and fix any faults by testing the questionnaire first.

While secondary market research may be quick and cheap, there are also factors that affect the accuracy of the data, as shown in the table below.

Sampling error	The original research may not have had the same target audience, so the data may be collected from a different perspective.
Bias in original analysis	The original analysis may have had differing influencing factors which may have distorted the analysis of the raw data, creating misleading secondary data.
Out of date data	Statistics and factual data may change quickly as external factors affect market conditions and trends.

 Recap

There is often a great deal of **raw data** from surveys, interviews and other sources. This data needs to be converted into a format this is easy to understand and analyse. This data can be summarized in different formats depending on the purpose of the data.

3.2.2 Presenting and using market research results

Tables, charts and graphs

Tables

Tables are useful for showing series of numerical data. They usually contain descriptions and lists and quantitative values. Tables are not useful for showing qualitative data.

Average weekly expenditure per household on goods and services, New Zealand ($)

Main product groups	2013
Food and drink	192.50
Clothing and footwear	31.60
Housing and household utilities	272.90
Household contents and services	27.10
Health	48.80
Transport	158.30
Communication	35.80
Recreation and culture	107.20
Education	18.40
Other	218.80
Total	1111.40

Source: Household Economic Survey, Statistics New Zealand

Charts and graphs

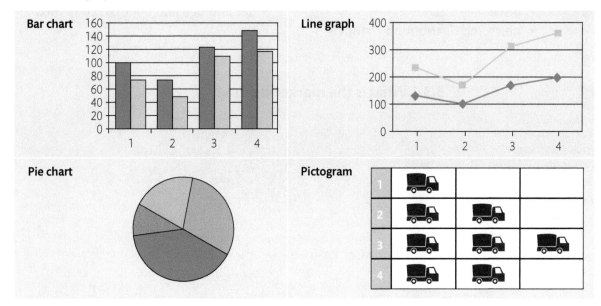

Figure 3.19 *Think carefully about how to present data – does your chart or graph demonstrate the important points in your data?*

Charts and graphs are useful for presenting quantitative data visually. Totals, amounts and changes can be easily compared over time. Bar charts and line graphs are useful for showing the relationship between two or more different sets of data.

Pie charts are used to visualize the different proportions of a whole value. The bigger the slice, the bigger the proportion of the whole value.

Exam tip

Y axes (going up and down) are used to show quantity, and X axes (going across) are used to show what data is being measured.

Worked example

Identify two methods of displaying data visually. (2)

Pie charts and line graphs.:

Apply

Create a questionnaire in your class on a subject you are interested in and then display the data in a visual poster display.

Review

Before you continue, make sure you are able to:

- describe and explain the role of market research and the different methods used

- describe and explain the different methods of primary and secondary research

- present and analyse market research results, drawing conclusions from data.

You need to know:
- product
- price
- place and distribution channels
- promotion
- technology and the marketing mix.

3.3.1 What is the marketing mix?

Recap

There are many reasons why customers buy products and services. However, four main factors make up the **marketing mix**, as shown in Figure 3.20.

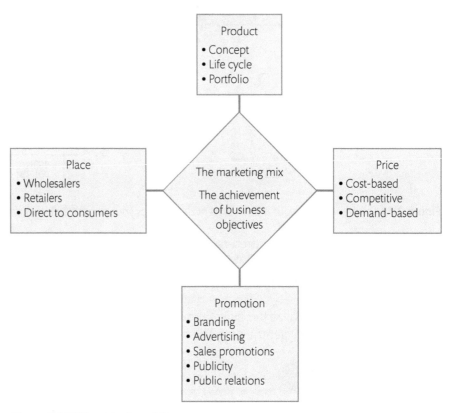

Product
- Concept
- Life cycle
- Portfolio

Place
- Wholesalers
- Retailers
- Direct to consumers

The marketing mix

The achievement of business objectives

Price
- Cost-based
- Competitive
- Demand-based

Promotion
- Branding
- Advertising
- Sales promotions
- Publicity
- Public relations

Figure 3.20 *What's in the mix?*

These different elements work together to create a marketing strategy to create a customer want for a particular product.

3.3.2 Product

Recap

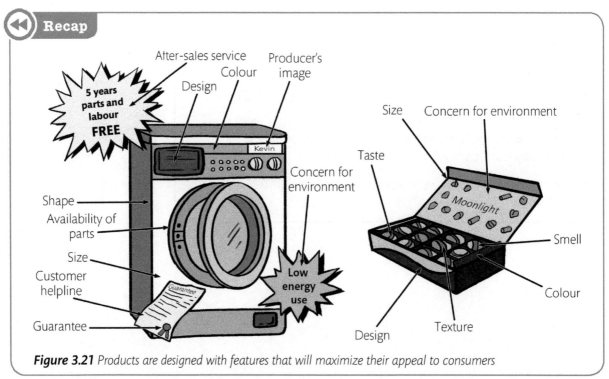

Figure 3.21 *Products are designed with features that will maximize their appeal to consumers*

The product is often considered to be the most important part of the marketing mix. This is because:

- it does not matter how good the packaging is if the product does not meet the need of the consumer

- the product needs to be fit for purpose and fulfill the role intended – poor design or unreliability may damage the reputation of the product and the business

- the product components must meet the target audience and match their ability to purchase.

Product development

To stay competitive, businesses must develop new products. This can mean:

- redesigning previous version

- creating new products.

A new product must fulfill at least one of the following criteria:

- meet a gap in the market

- be a noticeable improvement on the previous version

- be benchmarked against competitors to ensure additional features.

The costs of developing products are high, so effective market research is necessary in order to minimize the risk of product failure.

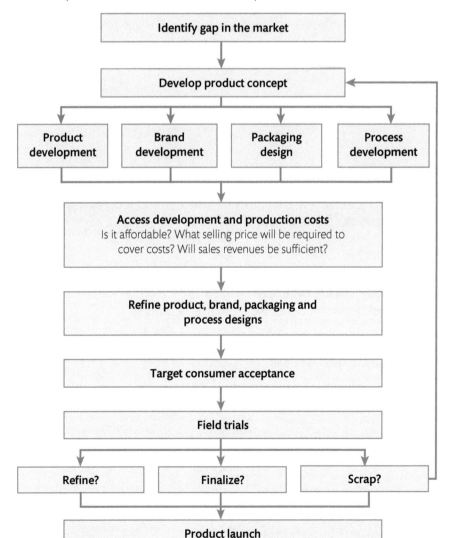

Figure 3.22 A typical product development flow chart

Exam tip

Field trials are often used with new products to identify potential weaknesses and problems to minimize the risk of damage to the brand.

Figure 3.24 *Packaging must protect products, provide information and appeal to consumers.*

 Apply

Choose some examples of unfamiliar or foreign packaging and then challenge your friends to describe the brand, brand image and reputation based on the packaging and brand details available.

Packaging

As the packaging is often the first element of the product a customer notices, it must be appropriate. **Packaging** also fulfills other functions such as the ones shown in Figure 3.23.

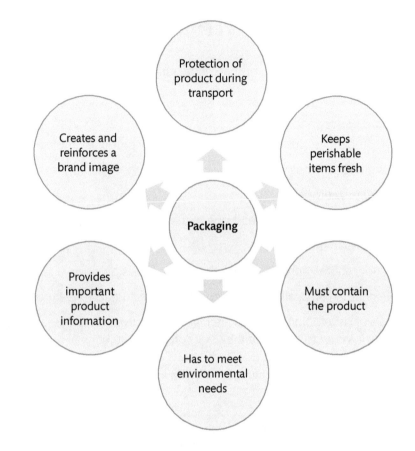

Figure 3.23 *Packaging serves a number of functions, and must be designed carefully*

Brand image

A **brand** is a name and/or image used to identify and distinguish a specific good, service or business from others. There are various other ways in which a brand can be identified.

The product life cycle

As one product is developed and 'born', another will be entering the decline stage of its **life cycle** (see Figure 3.25) and will eventually 'die'. A number of factors influence the lifespan of a product:

- changing consumer tastes
- technological advancement
- social and environmental factors
- levels of competition.

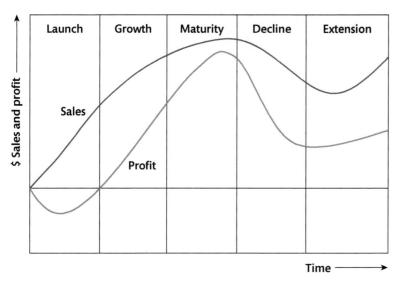

Figure 3.25 *A typical product life cycle*

	Launch	Growth	Maturity	Decline
	Low	*Rising*	*At a peak*	*Falling*
Objective	Increase product awareness	Build brand loyalty and compete effectively	Maintain brand loyalty	Product or business survival
Product	Offer one version	Add new versions	Offer a full product range	Keep best-sellers, scrap the rest
Price and competition	Price low to create sales	Price competitively to build market share as competition increases	Defend market share and profits from competitors	Adjust prices to stay profitable
Place	Use limited outlets	Increase places to buy	Expand methods and places of sale to their maximum	Reduction in number of retailers willing to sell the product
Promotion	Use informative advertising to build awareness	Use persuasive advertising to build brand loyalty	Remind consumers of product qualities	Reduce to a minimum or introduce an extension strategy

Extension strategies can be used to prolong the life of a product. This is usually done with products which have high brand recognition and an established market position.

Possible extension strategies are shown in Figure 3.26.

Product portfolios

As businesses develop and become successful, they can expand from a single product to a number of products or into new markets.

This **diversification** into new products or new markets has some beneficial effects on businesses:

• reduces the risk of overall business failure if one product fails

• increases the brand awareness of a business

• increases the revenue of a business.

Figure 3.26 *Extension strategies help extend the product life cycle*

Worked example

What is meant by 'branding'? (2)

Branding is creating distinctive and long-lasting perceptions of a product in the minds of the customer.

 Recap

When a business sets the **price** of a product, they must make sure that the price set meets three conditions:

- the price will (eventually) cover the production, marketing and selling costs, while leaving a profit
- the price considers the amount of competition
- the price is acceptable for the target audience.

3.3.3 Price

Factors influencing pricing decisions

There are three main factors that need to be considered when setting the price:

- the cost of production and level of profit required
- the amount of competition
- the level and strength of consumer demand.

Once a business is aware of these factors, it must then consider the influences shown in Figure 3.27.

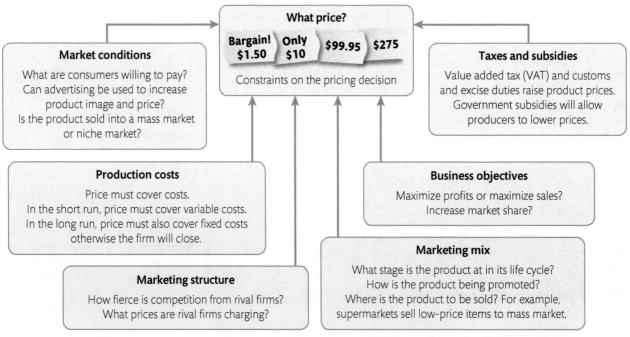

Figure 3.27 *Influences on the pricing decision*

Pricing methods

There are many different methods a business can choose when setting a price. The methods chosen will depend on many factors, including:

- the stage of the product's life cycle
- brand awareness
- the business objectives.

The main pricing strategies are shown in the table below.

Pricing strategy	Definition	Benefits	Limitations
Cost-plus	$\left(\dfrac{Total\ cost}{Total\ output}\right)$ + percentage mark-up or fixed amount	Ensures costs covered and profit made Easy to calculate and respond to changes in costs	Does not take into account customer requirements Does not take into consideration competitor pricing
Competitive destruction pricing (undercutting)	Benchmarking against a competitor price	Ensures a business can compete on price Useful for price-sensitive customers Can meet the requirements of the market	Price may not cover production costs Customers may not be price sensitive Incorrect or flawed competitor pricing Can start destructive price wars
Penetration	Setting low initial prices (may be below average cost of production)	Quick to build customer base Fast sales growth and increased market share Keeps costs low May force other businesses out of the market	Sacrifices profit for market share and brand awareness May not gain loyal customers who will pay 'normal' prices
Skimming	Charging a high initial price to cover research and development costs in a monopolistic market	High profits Covers research and development costs quickly Takes advantage of early adopters	Unsuitable for competitive markets Only early adopters will buy while most will wait for the price to fall
Promotion	Setting low prices for a short period of time to boost customer interest	Increases product sales Expands customer base quickly Takes market share from competitors	Profit sacrificed for revenue May start a price war May only attract short-term price-sensitive customers

 Worked example

Identify and explain two pricing strategies. (4)

One pricing strategy is cost-plus pricing. This is where you work out the cost and then add a fixed percentage or amount on top. A second strategy is price skimming. This is setting a high initial price to maximize short-term profits when there is little competition.

Peak travel per day
Old fare: $4
Number of passengers: 100
Total revenue: = $400

New fare: $5
Number of passengers: 95
Total revenue: = $475

Off-peak travel per day
Old fare: $2
Number of passengers: 50
Total revenue: = $125

New fare: $2.50
Number of passengers: 40
Total revenue: = $100

Exam tip

You will not be assessed on your ability to calculate price-elastic demand.

 Recap

It is very important to choose the most efficient and effective method of distribution for your product or service.
Distribution is getting the right product to the right consumer, at the right time and in the right quantity.

Price elasticity

Price elasticity may be used to influence pricing decisions if the ultimate goal is to increase revenue and/or profit.

Price elasticity shows the responsiveness of consumer demand to a change in price.

Reasons for price elasticity	Reasons for price inelasticity
Less competition	There are few substitutes
Lower costs as product quality is more important than advertising	Low-cost items where the price is insignificant
Attracts high-value customers	When goods are necessities, not luxuries
Creates a reputation of specialism	

Price-elastic demand is:

- when a small increase in the price of a product causes a significant fall in total demand and sales, or
- when a small decrease in the price of a product causes a significant rise in total demand and sales.

Price inelastic demand is:

- when a small increase in the price of a product causes a small fall in total demand and sales, or
- when a small decrease in the price of a product causes a small rise in total demand and sales.

3.3.4 Place

Distribution channels

There are many different elements that businesses need to consider when planning the most appropriate **distribution channel** (see Figure 3.28).

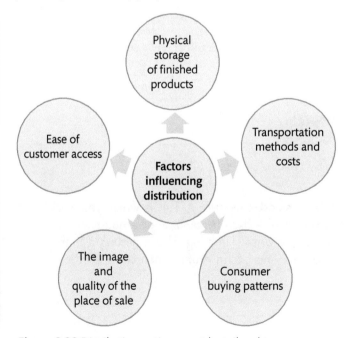

Figure 3.28 *Distribution options must be tailored to consumers, quality and cost*

There are many different channels of **distribution** that businesses may use, as shown in Figure 3.29.

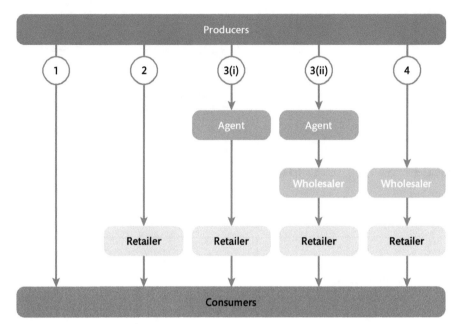

Figure 3.29 *Channels of distribution to consumers*

Each distribution channel has its own benefits and drawbacks, as shown in the table below.

Distribution method	Common examples	Benefits	Drawbacks
Direct from producer to consumer	Retail outlets owned by the producer; online or mail order	Retain full control of distribution channel Build close customer relationships Lower distribution costs Low-cost advertising online	Large cost of bulk deliveries Large investment into infrastructure Online sales may have large courier costs
Indirect through retailers	Retail outlets owned by third parties who stock more than one brand; supermarkets	Ability to sell large quantities Retailers often have their own distribution channels which reduces costs Retailers often help promote goods	No control over selling price and strategy No relationship with final customers Higher selling price due to retailer costs
Indirect through agents	Agents who earn commission on every good sold; travel agents, foreign agents with local knowledge	Agents have detailed, specialist knowledge	Less control over distribution and sales Commission adds to the final selling price
Indirect through wholesalers	Businesses who buy in bulk from many manufacturers and break bulk deliveries into smaller quantities for retailers	Wholesalers buy in bulk and pay for storage Cost of distribution borne by wholesaler Reduces time and cost of making sales	Less control of distribution and sales to final customer Higher selling price due to wholesaler costs Takes longer to reach customers

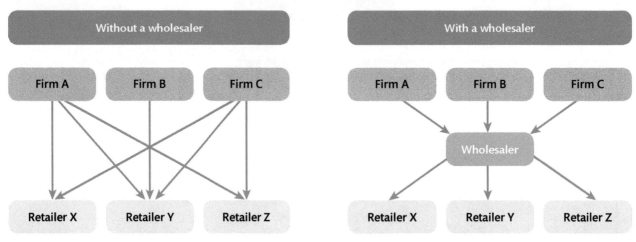

Figure 3.30 *The function of a wholesaler*

	Is the product luxury or standard?	• Luxury goods may require direct sales to maintain high standards • Standard goods are more suitable to indirect sales
	Is the product unique or specialized?	• Unique goods require direct sales to ensure specifications • Standard or mass-market goods may be bought indirect
	How urgent is the delivery?	• Just-in-time and perishable goods require direct sales

Figure 3.31 *Factors that affect the choice of distribution channel*

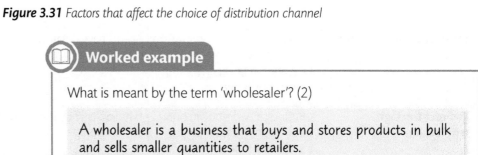

Worked example

What is meant by the term 'wholesaler'? (2)

A wholesaler is a business that buys and stores products in bulk and sells smaller quantities to retailers.

Choosing the most effective method of transport

When producing and selling a good it is important to choose the most effective method of transporting your product.

The two main factors to consider are:

• speed of delivery

• cost of delivery.

Delivery lead time is an important consideration as customers increasingly require fast delivery at a low cost. It is also important to consider whether the good is perishable (such as food) and requires fast transport.

3.3.5 Promotion

While the main aim of **promotion** is to raise consumer awareness of a product, there are also other reasons businesses use promotion, as shown in Figure 3.32.

Figure 3.32 *Promotions serve an important purpose in the generation of both profit and new customers*

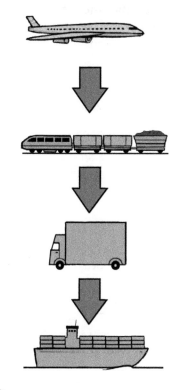

Recap

Promotions are marketing communication designed to influence customer behaviour and spending decisions.

The two main types of advertising

There are many different methods of advertising as highlighted on pages 86 and 87. Each of these fulfills either one or both aims of advertising:

1. **Informative advertising**

    • to provide relevant information

    • to provide factual information

    • to increase product credibility and desirability.

2. **Persuasive advertising**

    • to create a customer want

    • to boost sales of a particular product

    • to meet target segment requirements

    • to create and reinforce a brand image.

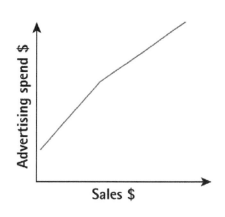

Brand loyalty

If advertising and promotions are successful, consumers may become brand loyal. There are many benefits of **brand loyalty** including:

- repeat purchases from loyal customers
- may reduce the impact of price cuts from competitors
- protects market share from competitors
- customers may be willing to pay a higher price for a particular branded good
- reduces price elasticity of demand.

Methods of above-the-line promotion

> **Exam tip**
>
> **Above-the-line** promotions are communications using mass advertising media.

Advertising media	Advantages	Disadvantages
National newspapers NATIONAL NEWS	✓ Newspapers are bought by a large number of people. ✓ A lot of product information can be provided in an advertisement. ✓ Readers can keep the newspaper and refer back to an advertisement. ✓ It is reasonably inexpensive to advertise.	✗ Most newspapers are only in black and white. ✗ Small advertisements tend to get "lost" among others. ✗ Readers often ignore advertising sections. ✗ Sales are falling due to more online news.
Regional and local newspapers LOCAL NEWS	✓ Advertisements can be linked to local products, features and events. ✓ Advertisements can be used to test market promotions before national launch.	✗ Most of these are only in black and white and reproduction can be poor. ✗ The average cost per reader is relatively high due to limited circulation.
Magazines Business Focus	✓ Advertisements can be linked to featured articles. ✓ Advertisements can be targeted at specific magazines and the consumers who read them, for example, gardening, travel, sports and car magazines.	✗ Advertisements often have to be submitted a long time before publication. ✗ Magazines may only be published weekly or monthly. ✗ Advertising in magazines is more expensive than in newspapers. ✗ Competitors' products are often displayed on the same page.
Radio	✓ Creative use can be made of sound, including music. ✓ Advertisements are relatively cheap to produce and broadcast. ✓ There are a growing number of digital stations. ✓ Advertisements can be targeted at different stations and audiences, for example, younger people listening to pop music stations.	✗ Visual messages cannot be broadcast. ✗ The advertisement is often short-lived. ✗ Consumers may not listen to advertisements. ✗ Radio has more limited audiences than national newspapers and television.

Advertising media	Advantages	Disadvantages
Television	✓ Creative use can be made of moving images, colour, music and sound. ✓ There are large audiences. ✓ Repeats can reinforce messages. ✓ Advertisements can be targeted at different audiences by type of programme, for example, for insurance and security systems during police dramas.	✗ Production and broadcast costs are high, especially at peak times. ✗ Advertising messages are usually short-lived. ✗ Television audiences may use advertising breaks in programmes for other activities, for example, to make a drink or go to the toilet.
Movies (including new releases at cinemas, on disc and online)	✓ Creative use can be made of moving images, colour, music and other sound. ✓ Advertisements can be targeted at different audiences by type of movie, for example, advertising toys, fizzy drinks and sweets during cartoon movies.	✗ These have more limited audiences than television and some other media. ✗ Messages cannot be reinforced by repeat showings.
Posters and billboards SALE NOW ON!!	✓ These offer cheap and permanent displays. ✓ They can be placed in areas where many people drive or walk by or where people have to wait, such as platforms at train stations.	✗ Messages can be missed as people often ignore them or pass by very quickly. ✗ Posters and billboards can only provide limited information. ✗ They are susceptible to vandalism and adverse weather conditions.
The internet	✓ It is easy and relatively cheap to develop a website and sell products online. ✓ Websites can deliver information in an attractive way to large numbers of potential consumers all over the world. ✓ Up-to-date and personalized promotional messages and product offers can be targeted at different groups of consumers using emails and via social media, including Facebook and Twitter.	✗ Internet access is limited in some countries. ✗ There are many competing websites. ✗ Search engines and comparison sites may not highlight a website. ✗ Online credit card fraud may discourage customers from buying online.
Leaflets	✓ This is a cheap form of advertising, especially for small, local businesses such as restaurants and repair shops. ✓ Leaflets can be handed out to a wide range of potential customers near the business. ✓ Leaflets can contain discount codes or money-off coupons to encourage people to keep and use them to make purchases.	✗ Many leaflets can be wasted: people may not read them or may throw them away in the street creating litter and a poor reputation for the business. ✗ Leaflets delivered door to door may be considered "junk mail", annoying customers and thereby putting them off using the business or buying the product advertised.
Other YOUR LOGO HERE	✓ Other methods include inexpensive forms of advertising, for example, logos and messages on carrier bags, T-shirts or other products.	✗ Advertisements may not be seen by consumers in target markets. ✗ It is possible to send a negative message, for example, if lots of carrier bags bearing a logo or message are discarded.

Methods of below-the-line promotion

Advertising media		Uses of below-the-line
Publicity e.g. sales literature, signage, product endorsements, product placement, trade shows		Pulls the customer into the store in a relatively cheap and easy fashion
Public relations e.g. sponsorship, donations, press releases		Useful to repair a damaged brand or maintain a positive image through association with popular culture
Sales incentives e.g. money-off coupons, competitions, loyalty cards, bonuses		Aimed at creating customer loyalty by providing incentives to continue buying the product
Direct mail		Can be personalized from databases to promote and provide information in a low-cost manner
Personal selling		Personalize the final sale of high-value goods by discussing features and specifications
Aftersales care		Reassures customers if a fault occurs that the customer will be protected and not out of pocket

The need for cost effectiveness in marketing budgets

Promotions can be expensive. It is important that the amount of money spent on promotion is not more than the anticipated revenue, as this may cause the business to fail.

To ensure that spending is controlled, businesses create marketing budgets.

These financial plans estimate the likely costs over a period of time and aim to ensure marketing is cost effective.

Marketing budget

Market research costs include:
- design, preparation and analysis
- conducting interviews and surveys
- test marketing
- subscriptions to secondary sources.

General marketing expenses include:
- advertising agency commissions
- salaries for marketing managers
- salaries for marketing assistants
- office space
- fixtures and fittings
- travel costs.

Marketing communications costs include:
- printing and mailing
- development of a brand's logo
- developing and hosting a website
- designing a brochure
- radio, television and cinema advertising
- direct marketing
- newspaper advertising
- attending events
- personal selling
- PR
- sponsorships and donations
- sales incentives, including competitions.

 Worked example

Identify and explain two possible methods of above-the-line promotion. (6)

> One method is using national newspapers, as they reach a large number of people. Another method is using radio, as the business could devise a catchy slogan which people will hear, remember and associate with the product.

 Apply

Create a promotional resource for your favourite snack, targeting a specific audience and ask your friends to guess who the target audience is.

3.3.6 Technology and the marketing mix

Recap

New technology such as e-commerce, the internet, social media and robotics and automation are transforming business planning and implementation.

PRODUCT

Technological change has created new consumer wants and products to satisfy them, including smartphones and satellite navigators. Many product life cycles are becoming shorter.

A new product can now be designed using 3D software and manufactured by computer-controlled machines.

PRICE

Prices of items sold online can be adjusted quickly as market conditions change using dynamic pricing. For example, the price of holidays on specific dates can be reduced if they fail to sell out in time.

Price discounts can be targeted at different consumers to encourage their purchases using email and coupon websites.

PLACE

Many businesses now sell their products direct to their customers and take payment for their purchases over the internet.

Service providers, such as banks and insurance companies, are also able to offer their services direct to customers online.

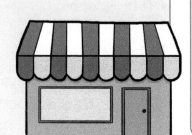

PROMOTIONS

Websites provide "shop windows" for the products of businesses that are "open" every hour of every day to consumers all over the world.

Businesses can also promote their products through "pop-up" adverts on the websites of online retailers, for example, Amazon, or on social networking sites such as Facebook.

The internet and e-commerce

E-commerce can reduce marketing costs, increase brand control and increase the sales of a business.

E-commerce can be used to promote and sell products and services direct to the consumer.

Search engines including Google, Bing and Baidu enable customers to search and compare through websites to find the best prices for the specific product required.

Advantages of e-commerce to businesses	Disadvantages of e-commerce to businesses
✓ Websites are a cheap way of marketing and selling to consumers all over the world.	✗ It increases competition between businesses, including with firms located overseas. Domestic firms may lose custom and revenue.
✓ A business can attract more customers through a website than through using other methods.	✗ Increased competition may force some shops and shopping chains to close down.
✓ It saves money buying or renting retail outlets and on the employment of retail staff.	✗ Staff will need to be trained to maintain and update websites and to deal with online ordering, payments and distribution.
✓ Businesses can search for low-cost providers of the goods and services they need.	✗ Businesses must protect themselves from online fraud and credit card scams. If they do not, it may stop customers from shopping online.
✓ Information about customers and their purchasing histories can be recorded easily and used to target email promotions about product offers and discounts to different customers.	✗ Website design and maintenance costs can be high.

Advantages of e-commerce to consumers	Disadvantages of e-commerce to consumers
✓ Consumers can choose to buy from a wider variety of goods and services and from a greater number of suppliers based in different countries. ✓ Increased competition between businesses using e-commerce can help to reduce prices and improve product quality and customer services. ✓ Consumers need not spend so much time and money travelling to shops. This can also help reduce road congestion and pollution.	✗ Increasing online shopping may force local shops to close. Consumers without internet access will have less choice and may have to travel further to shops. ✗ Consumers may have to take time off work to accept deliveries of goods purchased online. ✗ It may be more difficult to return damaged or faulty goods than to simply take them back to a shop. ✗ Despite security measures, online fraud is rising. Consumers' personal credit card and bank details are being stolen and misused by online criminal hackers. ✗ Consumers may receive irritating and unwanted email promotions and spam emails.

Social networking

Social media is fast overtaking television, the internet and radio as a means of advertising.

Social media is a fast and low-cost method of two-way communication with customers.

There are many ways in which social media can be used (see Figure 3.33).

> **Exam tip**
>
> Businesses do not advertise on the internet – businesses advertise on websites, social media and pages on the internet.

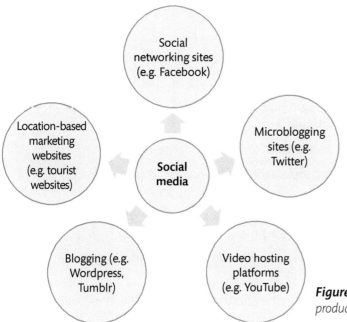

Figure 3.33 Social media plays a growing role in the promotion of products and services

Advantages of using social media	Disadvantages of using social media
✓ It is a cost-effective way of reaching a large number of potential customers around the world. ✓ Many forms of social media allow businesses to target specific groups, often in particular locations. ✓ Many forms of social media are free. ✓ Promotional messages can be updated quickly and easily as market conditions change. ✓ Consumers in the target market will see the marketing messages and advertisements as soon as they enter social networking sites. ✓ Messages can be personalized and two-way, allowing customers to correspond directly with the business thereby creating good customer relationships and loyalty.	✗ Some consumers may find pop-ups and constant messaging from many different businesses annoying and may ignore them. ✗ Pop-up advertisements need to be paid for and can be expensive. Businesses also have less control over how their advertisements are displayed by the host site. ✗ Some promotional messages may be changed by social media users and forwarded on to others with the intention of ridiculing a business and damaging its reputation. ✗ The governments of some countries restrict the use of social media.

Worked example

Explain two types of social media a business could use. Recommend which would be the most useful. Justify your answer. (6)

A business could use a social networking site such as Facebook and a microblogging service, as products are targeting younger technical customers, which means the business could have conversations with large numbers of people and also send short messages to potential customers. A social networking site would be most useful, as customers can easily share links and the business could target a wide range of potential customers easily, cheaply and quickly.

Review

Before you continue, make sure you are able to:

- describe and explain the concept of brands and the product life cycle
- identify and explain some costs and benefits of developing new products
- describe and explain the role of packaging
- draw and interpret a product life-cycle diagram
- identify and explain how stages of the product life cycle can influence marketing decisions
- understand and explain how pricing decisions are made
- understand and explain the significance and importance of price elasticity
- describe and explain the importance of different distribution channels and the factors that affect their selection
- describe and explain the role and aims of promotion and the different forms used
- describe and explain the importance of marketing budgets
- understand and explain the impact of technology including e-commerce and its opportunities and threats
- identify and explain the uses of the internet and social networks for promotion.

You need to know:
- how to decide which marketing strategies appropriate for a given situation
- the nature and impact of legal controls related to marketing
- the opportunities and problems of entering new foreign markets.

3.4.1 Developing marketing strategies

A marketing strategy combines all the elements of the marketing mix. Marketing strategies depend on market conditions, the size of the business and its competitors, and the strength of consumer demand.

Examples of marketing strategies

The main marketing strategies exist to meet the aims shown in Figure 3.34.

 Recap

A **marketing strategy** identifies the marketing objectives of a business and the actions and resources needed to achieve them.

Figure 3.34 *Marketing strategies are defined by their objectives, which differ from business to business and product to product*

Businesses use models such as **SWOT analysis** to predict future changes that may affect marketing strategies.

As they are often long term, marketing strategies must be flexible and respond to changeable market conditions (Figure 3.35).

Exam tip

A SWOT analysis is an analysis of the internal **s**trengths and **w**eaknesses of a business and the external **o**pportunities and **t**hreats.

Economic influences on customer buying habits

Market conditions

The maturity of a product range

New technologies may change current buying habits

Figure 3.35 *Building a long-term marketing strategy involves making it resilient to changing market conditions*

Worked example

What is meant by the term 'marketing strategy'? (2)

> A marketing strategy is a plan detailing the objectives of a business and the resources needed to achieve them.

3.4.2 Legal controls on marketing

Different countries have different laws on what advertising is allowed and what is not allowed.

Protection of consumers

Common consumer protection laws protect against:

- unsafe goods or services
- goods that do not match the advertised claims
- goods that do not meet regulations on quality and/or condition
- false written and verbal product descriptions
- using inaccurate measurements
- failing to identify and explain hidden feeds, charges or taxes
- unhygienic preparation conditions
- offensive or indecent advertising.

The impact of complying with consumer law

Complying with consumer law often increases the costs of a business, as shown in Figure 3.36.

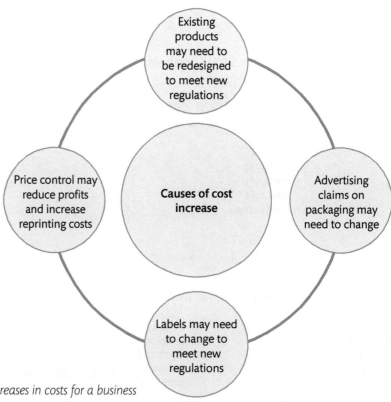

Figure 3.36 *Legal issues can cause increases in costs for a business*

However, there are also many benefits of complying with consumer law (Figure 3.37).

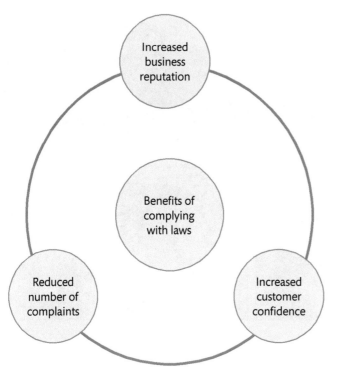

Figure 3.37 *Compliance also benefits businesses, and can lead to greater profit, market share and expansion*

3.4.3 Marketing in foreign markets

As existing markets reach saturation levels, new markets must be found to increase sales and profit.

Growth potential of new markets

Selling goods and services to customers in foreign countries can lead to growth for the reasons shown in Figure 3.38.

Figure 3.38 *Business growth*

Problems faced with foreign markets

- Small businesses may not speak foreign languages
- Problems with translating marketing materials

Language barriers

Different cultures, customs and tastes

- Easy to offend target audience without knowing
- Existing businesses have market dominance

- Can affect costs and revenues
- May reduce the value of sales and profits if exchange rates fall

Exchange rate risks

Different legal controls and taxes

- Some products may contain banned substances
- May affect business practices and advertising

Figure 3.39 *Expanding into international markets comes with risks, and requires careful planning*

 **Worked example**

Identify and explain two possible problems a business may encounter when entering foreign markets. (4)

One problem may be the language barrier. Terminology and slogans may not translate in the way intended and cause offence. Another problem is different laws and regulations. Businesses may need to alter the products to meet local regulations.

Overcoming problems when entering foreign markets

Businesses must reduce the risk of entering **foreign markets** to make sure the business venture is profitable. Some of the methods used are shown in Figure 3.40.

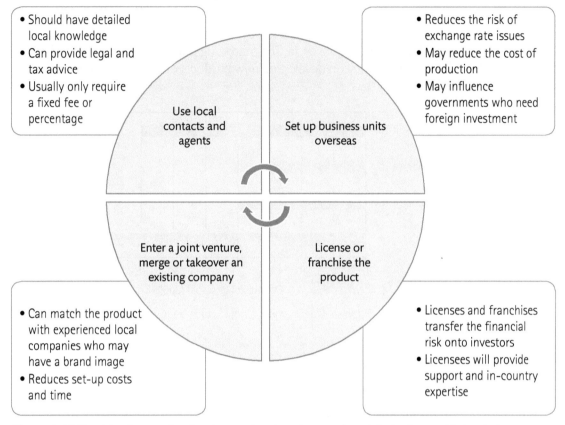

- Should have detailed local knowledge
- Can provide legal and tax advice
- Usually only require a fixed fee or percentage

Use local contacts and agents

Set up business units overseas

- Reduces the risk of exchange rate issues
- May reduce the cost of production
- May influence governments who need foreign investment

Enter a joint venture, merge or takeover an existing company

License or franchise the product

- Can match the product with experienced local companies who may have a brand image
- Reduces set-up costs and time

- Licenses and franchises transfer the financial risk onto investors
- Licensees will provide support and in-country expertise

Figure 3.40 *The risks of expanding into international markets can be minimized or avoided entirely*

Review

Before you continue, make sure you are able to:

- identify and explain the need for marketing strategies in business
- identify and describe the influences of different elements of the marketing mix
- recommend and justify appropriate marketing strategies for different situations
- describe and explain legal controls on marketing strategy
- describe and explain the opportunities and problems faced by businesses when entering new foreign markets
- describe and explain the growth potential of new markets
- identify the benefits and limitations of methods of overcoming problems.

Exam tip

As with all investments, it is important to ensure that market research has been carried out to reduce the risks of expansion.

Apply

Create a short news video or radio news clip identifying the problems a foreign business has faced when entering your country.

Exam-style questions

Unit 3

Toycroft makes children's toys. It operates in a very competitive market. The marketing manager believes that because Toycroft has high brand loyalty, demand for its toys is price inelastic.

The best-selling product is a soft toy, but as it is an old design, it is near the end of its product life cycle. The marketing manager has to decide whether to spend money on developing new products or use extension strategies for the soft toy.

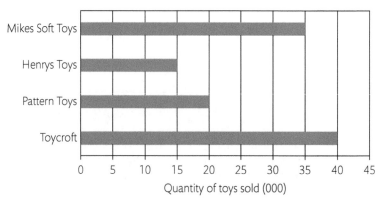

Figure 3.41 *Graph showing number of toys sold by four manufacturers*

(a) What is meant by 'brand loyalty'? (2)

(b) Calculate Toycroft's market share in 2018. (2)

(c) Define the term 'product life cycle'. (2)

(d) Explain the term 'marketing'. (2)

(e) Explain the term 'extension strategy'. (2)

(f) Explain two possible effects on Toycroft if the price of its products is increased. (4)

(g) Identify two extension strategies Toycroft could use. (4)

(h) Identify and explain two advantages of using extension strategies for Toycroft. (6)

(i) Do you think Toycroft should develop new products? Justify your answer. (6)

Unit 4:
Operations management

Unit outline

Without a product or service to sell, a business will not have any business activity, nor will it have any means of gaining revenue to pay the people in the business.

It is therefore important to understand how businesses make decisions about production and production methods, and how these affect the **operations management** of a business.

Your revision checklist

Either tick these boxes to build a record of your revision, **or** use them to identify your strengths and weaknesses.

Specification	Theme	🙂	😐	🙁
4.1 Production of goods and services	4.1.1 The meaning of production			
	4.1.2 The main methods of production			
	4.1.3 How technology has changed production methods			
4.2 Costs, scale of production and break-even analysis	4.2.1 The identification and classification of costs			
	4.2.2 Economies and diseconomies of scale			
	4.2.3 Break-even analysis			
4.3 Achieving quality production	4.3.1 Why quality is important and how quality production might be achieved			
4.4 Location decisions	4.4.1 The main factors influencing the location and relocation decisions of a business			

4.1.1 The meaning of production

Many businesses produce products for sale. The best businesses manage their resources effectively to produce goods and services that satisfy customer demand.

Production and productivity

Production is the process of turning raw materials (**inputs**) into products ready for sale to the customer (**outputs**). This process is called adding value – making the value of the finished product worth more than the total value of the raw materials (including labour).

The total value of production (output) can be measured in two ways:

1. The volume of all goods or services produced within a specific time period

2. The value of all goods produced within a specific time period.

The method of measurement depends on the type of products the business is producing:

- higher value goods produced at lower quantities are often measured by value

- Lower priced, mass-produced goods are often measured by the volume of output.

Apply

Choose a business and challenge your colleagues to identify the best method of production. Ask them to explain their choice.

While production is the process of producing, productivity is the method used to measure the amount produced from a certain amount of input.

Pakistan		China		USA	
20m	33m	15m	37m	9.1m	84m
1.65 tonnes per cow		2.47 tonnes per cow		9.23 tonnes per cow	

If productivity increases, a business can produce more products with fewer inputs. This increases efficiency and leads to decreased costs and increased profits.

Businesses often try to increase productivity by making employees produce more in the same time period. This reduces labour costs, which are often a business's biggest cost.

Figure 4.1a *Productive*   **Figure 4.1b** *More productive*

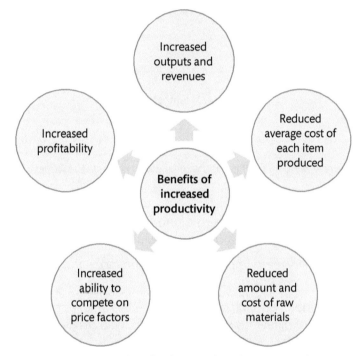

Figure 4.2 *Businesses benefit when productivity is increased*

Labour productivity

Productivity is not used to measure individuals; it measures the average productivity per worker, per period.

In businesses which rely on human labour as the main factor of production of goods, labour productivity is the most common measure used.

The calculation for **labour productivity** is:

$$Average\ productivity\ of\ labour = \frac{total\ output}{number\ of\ employees}$$

Where the business produces services, labour productivity is difficult to measure as there may be many different types of employees necessary.

Therefore, it is better to measure the average revenue per worker, per period.

$$Average\ revenue\ productivity\ of\ labour = \frac{total\ output}{number\ of\ employees}$$

It may be difficult to measure organizations that do not produce goods or services for sale. Therefore, other performance measures must be used which are specific to the organization (see Figure 4.3).

Exam tip

Remember that some methods of increasing labour productivity may have unwanted effects, such as a decrease in quality.

Figure 4.3 *Productivity is not the only way to measure the success of a business*

Increasing efficiency

As productivity increases, the costs of production are reduced. However, there are other costs which must be considered, such as:

- training employees to improve their performance – this means that production levels drop in the short term
- replacing employees with outdated skills – this requires redundancy and recruitment of differently skilled employees, who may require a higher wage or salary
- replacing existing machinery with updated technology – this may reduce short-term production levels.

Other methods of increasing productivity and **efficiency** include:

- self-reflection and streamlining operations, e.g. by reducing the product range, retaining only the most profitable options
- rewarding employees with performance-related pay
- improving the working environment and job satisfaction
- managing inventories effectively
- introducing lean production methods.

Worked example

Identify and explain two possible methods of increasing efficiency in a business. (4)

One method is to train employees, which will improve skills and abilities. A second method is to use mechanization, which reduces human mistakes and wasted resources.

Inventories

Inventories are the stocks of:

- raw materials
- works-in-progress
- finished goods.

Stored by a business to ensure constant production and meet customer demand, inventories are a part of a business's current **assets**.

If a business holds too little inventory, they are in danger of:

- having breaks in production, which leads to paying fixed costs with no output
- failing to meet spikes in customer demand and losing market share – the delivery lead time will be too long.

If a business holds too much stock, then they are in danger of affecting the rate of inventory turnover through overstocking.

Overstocking	The rate of inventory turnover
Holding excess **inventory** has the following disadvantages: × More cash is used up purchasing inventories leaving the business with less to pay other commitments. × More storage space must be used or rented by the business. × Work-in-progress and finished goods held in storage for a long time will lose value if they perish or go out of fashion: they may have to be sold at a loss or written off.	This measures how quickly inventory is used up in a business and therefore how quickly the item needs to be reordered and replaced. It will vary by the type of product and at different times each year.

Figure 4.4 *Expensive consumer durable items tend to have low rates of inventory turnover*

Lean production

Lean production is one of the most effective methods of increasing production efficiency: waste and inefficiency in the production process can be minimized by reducing the time, costs and materials used in the process.

A simple method of achieving these production efficiencies is to rearrange and reorganize the work space to increase usable production space and the production flow, while minimizing the time wasted by transporting materials.

The main principles of lean production are:

- continuous improvement in production processes
- speeding up the continuous flow of production
- reduction of waste and improvement of work quality.

The two main methods of lean production are **just-in-time** and **Kaizen**.

Figure 4.5 *Sweets have a very high rate of turnover during the Islamic festival of Eid due to increased demand*

Removing waste from production

Lean production recognizes seven types of waste that can occur in production. They involve:

- transportation: moving products around unnecessarily
- stocks: storing too many components, semi-finished and finished products
- motion: people or equipment moving or walking more than is required to perform a task
- waiting time: time wasted between each stage of the production process
- overproduction: producing more than is needed to meet customer demand
- over-processing: creating unnecessary activities due to poor equipment or product design
- defects: the effort involved in inspecting and fixing product defects.

Just-in-time

Just-in-time production relies on stockless production – a business holds little or no stocks of raw materials and relies on the efficient delivery of materials exactly when needed.

Advantages	Disadvantages
✓ Reductions in the cost of holding stock	✘ A delay in supplies can negatively affect production
✓ Warehouse space can be used for production or other income streams	✘ Dependence of the quality and reliability of suppliers
✓ Increased turnover, which leads to increased cash flow	✘ Needs suppliers to be located close by

Kaizen

Kaizen is the Japanese term for continuous improvement. It relies on all of the employees participating by identifying problems and making suggestions for solutions to improve productivity and reduce waste. Once a solution is found, this becomes part of the standard production process.

Advantages	Disadvantages
✓ Prevents the production of defective products	✘ Requires teamwork and a flat organizational structure
✓ Efficient use of labour and materials	✘ Requires motivated and skilled employees
✓ Improves employee motivation through greater participation	

Exam tip

Lean production is only a useful method of production if the business has a reliable supply chain.

4.1.2 The main methods of production

Production can be organized in a business in three main ways, depending on the type of product and the customer requirements: job production, batch production and flow (mass) production.

Job production

Key elements of **job production**:

- provides goods or services that are usually made or delivered to a specific order
- used for one-off, custom products or services
- difficult to reproduce the original item
- requires skilled craftspeople and specialized machinery for specific tasks.

Advantages	Disadvantages
✓ Products meet the precise requirements of their customers.	✗ It is labour-intensive and often takes a long time.
✓ Businesses can often include a premium in the price they charge their customers to reflect increased quality.	✗ Wage costs can be high.
	✗ As products are produced to order any mistakes can be expensive.
✓ Workers have varied jobs and many can make a finished product from start to finish. This can motivate workers and create a sense of pride in their work.	

Batch production

Key elements of **batch production**:

- produces a limited number of identical products to meet a specific customer order

- within each stage, work is completed on the whole batch before the next stage begins

- increased economies of scale to job production.

> **Exam tip**
>
> Job, batch and flow production may all use technology and machinery. However, the production methods are based on *how* the tools are used.

Advantages	Disadvantages
✓ It is a good way of adding variety to otherwise identical products in order to give consumers a wider choice, for example, producing a car with a choice of different colours and engine sizes.	✗ It needs careful planning to minimize the amount of unproductive time between different batches.
✓ Workers' tasks are more varied than in flow production, reducing the risk of boredom.	✗ Costs will be higher than for production on a mass scale.

Flow production

Key elements of **flow (mass) production**:

- a continuous production of identical or standardized products

- products are assembled, finished and packed on a continuously moving production line

- often automated and uses little labour.

See page 106 for advantages and disadvantages of flow production.

Advantages	Disadvantages
✓ Goods can be produced quickly and cheaply. Average costs per unit are lower due to economies of scale.	✘ The costs of equipment and machinery required to automate production lines can be high.
✓ Lower production costs can be passed on to consumers as lower prices help to boost demand and revenues.	✘ Storage requirements and the costs of stocks of materials, components and finished products can be substantial.
✓ Automated production lines can reduce the number of workers needed and cut labour costs.	✘ Machinery breakdowns, power cuts or supply problems with components will hold up production.
✓ Automated production can be continuous for 24 hours each day.	✘ Workers undertaking repetitive tasks may become bored.
✓ It allows workers to specialize in specific, repeated tasks.	

📖 Worked example

Identify two disadvantages of flow production. (2)

> One disadvantage is that the cost of machinery is high. Another disadvantage is there are large storage costs.

Choosing a method of production

It is important that businesses understand and meet the demands of the customer. The method of production may depend on a variety of factors (see Figure 4.6).

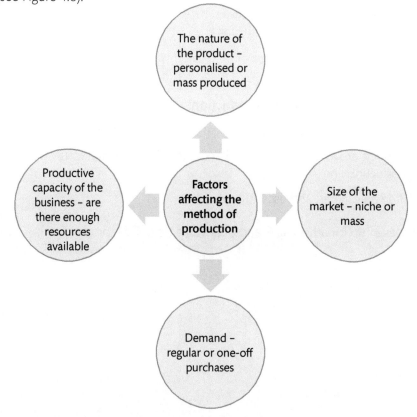

Figure 4.6 A variety of factors will influence the chosen method of production

4.1.3 How technology has changed production methods

Technology has created new materials, products and processes. This has influenced production methods. Where products may have been produced by people, they are now produced by machines.

While the price of computers and software has fallen dramatically, their power and speed has increased dramatically.

New processes

Computers are now able to assist and even control production process in the following methods:

1. **Computer-aided design (CAD)**

   • detailed and accurate drawings completed on computer programs

   • easily drawn, redrawn and altered

   • allows 3D modelling.

2. **Computer-aided manufacturing (CAM)**

   • computer-controlled robots complete processes without human operators

   • fast and accurate production process (no human error)

   • increased output, reduced waste, improved and standardized quality.

Spill overs of technology into different sectors

Technology developed for one use can often be easily used in different sectors, especially when patents have expired.

Technological **spill overs** are an external benefit, which means governments are keen to provide financial help to businesses that specialize in research and development of new technologies because of the following potential benefits:

• increase in manufacturing output of a country

• increased employment in hi-tech industries

• potential to create **disruptive technologies** that change entire markets and create new opportunities.

Replacement of labour

Labour input in many low-skilled or manufacturing jobs has been replaced by advanced machinery and production equipment due to:

• the reduction in the cost of advanced machinery

• the increased productivity of machinery over labour

• the increased complexity of machinery.

However, there are many factors that affect the ability of machinery to replace labour:

• machines cannot offer personalized care and services

• machinery is expensive to purchase and sometimes maintain.

• workers need retraining, which can take time and be expensive

• some customers do not want mass-produced goods.

Advantages of new technology to business	Disadvantages of new technology to business
✓ Firms can increase productivity and efficiency.	✗ Research and development of new products and processes can be expensive and not all will succeed.
✓ Labour costs can be reduced. Hi-tech businesses can recruit, train and manage fewer workers.	✗ The initial costs of buying or hiring new technologically advanced machines, like robots and other advanced equipment, can be high.
✓ Machines can be kept working all day, every day.	
✓ Product quality can be controlled and improved, resulting in less waste.	✗ Firms unwilling or unable to afford to invest in new technologies will lose custom to firms that do.
✓ The development of a new desirable product gives a firm a competitive advantage over others.	✗ Product life cycles are becoming shorter. This means businesses may earn less profit from each product and have to spend more money and time developing new ones.
✓ Consumers are replacing products and buying new ones more often to get the latest features.	
✓ Many modern technologies, such as computers, are affordable to even the smallest of firms.	✗ Workers may need to be retrained to use new materials, production processes and equipment.
✓ The internet and electronic communications allow information and payments to be exchanged easily, quickly and cheaply.	✗ Workers and trade unions may be reluctant to learn new skills, may resist changes in working practices and may even take strike action if the introduction of new technology threatens their jobs.
✓ Governments may offer tax and subsidy incentives to encourage investments in research and development and new technologies to boost economic growth.	

 Worked example

Exam tip

Technology does not just mean computers; technology means any development of existing and human-based processes.

What is meant by computer-aided design? (2)

> Computer-aided design is when complex parts and products are drawn on computer, which allows images to be seen in 3D.

 Review

Before you continue, make sure you are able to:

- understand the meaning of production
- explain how managing resources effectively is important for production
- explain the difference between production and productivity
- name the benefits and methods of increasing efficiency
- list the reasons for holding inventory
- explain the concept of lean production
- describe the main methods, features, benefits and limitations of production
- recommend and justify an appropriate production method for a given situation.

You need to know:
- how to identify and classify costs
- describe and use economies and diseconomies of scale
- how to use break-even analysis.

4.2.1 The identification and classification of costs

Costs are important to understand, because when costs are subtracted from revenue, they show the profit of a business.

Profit = total revenue − total costs

To control costs and become efficient, a business must identify all of the costs, calculate the total and set future target cost levels.

Types of cost

There are three main types of costs:

1. **Start-up costs**
   - all the premises, machinery, raw materials and other costs that are needed to start a business
   - As the business has not yet started selling anything, this must be paid for from capital investment as there are no revenues or profits.

2. **Fixed costs**
   - these do not vary with the amount of goods or services produced
   - may also be called overheads or indirect costs
   - includes the day to day running costs of a business

3. **Variable costs**
   - change directly with the amount of goods or services produced
   - may also be called direct costs as they are directly related to the product
   - pay for the specific materials used in the manufacture of a product.

   Total variable costs = variable costs per unit × total output

Average costs

A business must know how much each unit of output costs. This then allows the business to sell each unit at a profit.

$$\text{Average cost per unit} = \frac{\text{total cost}}{\text{total output}}$$

> **Exam tip**
>
> Remember that start-up costs are different from fixed and variable costs, and cannot be taken from profits (as there aren't any).

📖 Worked example

Identify and explain two fixed costs for a factory. (6)

One fixed cost is the rent of the factory, which is the same whether one or a hundred of the factory's products are made. Another fixed cost is the managers' salaries, which are the same even if they work overtime.

> **Exam tip**
>
> Remember to add both fixed and variable costs when calculating profit, as a common mistake is to use only the fixed or variable costs.

Using cost data to make decisions

It is essential to know total and average costs per unit. These help to make pricing decisions as they may answer some of the following questions:

- what selling price is needed to make a profit?
- what level of output is needed to cover business costs?
- what level of output is needed to produce a satisfactory level of profit?

Profit (or loss) per unit = selling price per unit – average cost per unit

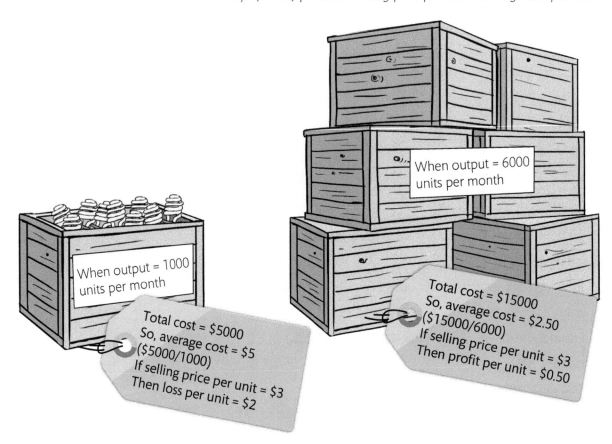

When output = 1000 units per month

Total cost = $5000
So, average cost = $5
($5000/1000)
If selling price per unit = $3
Then loss per unit = $2

When output = 6000 units per month

Total cost = $15000
So, average cost = $2.50
($15000/6000)
If selling price per unit = $3
Then profit per unit = $0.50

4.2.2 Economies and diseconomies of scale

Economies of scale

Economies of scale reduce the average cost of producing each unit of output as the scale of production is increased.

As more products are produced, the fixed cost per unit decreases as it is shared between a greater number of products. This is called **economies of scale**.

There are six main types of economies of scale that larger businesses are able to exploit:

1. **Purchasing economies**: Buying many products at once is often cheaper than buying fewer products many times. This is called **bulk buying**. Suppliers offer discounts as it is cheaper to make one large delivery than many small ones.

2. **Marketing economies:** As a business grows and has different or larger numbers of products for sale, the marketing costs can be shared between more units, which reduces the average cost of marketing per unit.

3. **Risk-bearing economies:** As a product has more markets, customers or products available, the business can reduce the risk of failure if one large customer is lost or if there is a fall in demand for one product.

4. **Technical economies:** Larger businesses can invest more capital and financial resources into specialized machinery and skilled employees which increases the efficiency of production.

5. **Financial economies:** Large businesses are able to borrow larger amounts of money at cheaper rates of interest than small businesses as they are considered to be less risky. Larger businesses that become limited companies are also able to sell shares in their business to investors.

6. **Managerial economies:** As a business expands, each department is able to employ specialist managers who are experts in their field. These can increase productivity and efficiency which reduces costs and increases output.

Diseconomies of scale

However, as businesses grow, they may become so large that they become less efficient, which results in average costs of production rising.

These **diseconomies of scale** occur when businesses need to invest in additional machines, equipment or factory space, which increases fixed costs.

The two main diseconomies of scale a business might suffer from are:

1. **Management diseconomies:** When a business has too many departments and layers of management there can be communication problems and disagreements. This may result in a slowdown in decision making, and instructions may take longer to reach workers.

2. **Labour diseconomies:** When employees work using mass-production methods they may become bored and demotivated from repetitive tasks and a lack of feeling valued. This may result in increased absenteeism and labour turnover, which may reduce productivity.

> **Exam tip**
>
> It is only an economy of scale if you intend to use all of the materials you buy.

> **Apply**
>
> Investigate your school and try to identify as many fixed and variable costs as you can. Can you find any economies of scale for your school? What would be the effects of your cost economies?

📖 Worked example

What is meant by 'diseconomy of scale'? (2)

> A diseconomy of scale is when a business grows so large that it becomes less efficient and average costs of production start to rise.

4.2.3 Break-even analysis

The concept of break-even

Before aiming to make a profit, a business must first make sure that it covers all the costs it has spent on production or providing services. A business must therefore aim to find out the minimum number of products or services it must sell to cover its costs.

This is called **break-even**. The formula for break-even is:

$$Total\ revenue = total\ cost$$

Output (units per month)	Fixed costs	Variable costs ($2 per unit)	Total costs	Total revenue ($3 per unit)	Profit or loss
0	$3000	0	$3000	0	−$3000
1000	$3000	$2000	$5000	$3000	−$2000
2000	$3000	$4000	$7000	$6000	−$1000
3000	$3000	$6000	$9000	$9000	0
4000	$3000	$8000	$11 000	$12 000	$1000
5000	$3000	$10 000	$13 000	$15 000	$2000
6000	$3000	$12 000	$15 000	$18 000	$3000

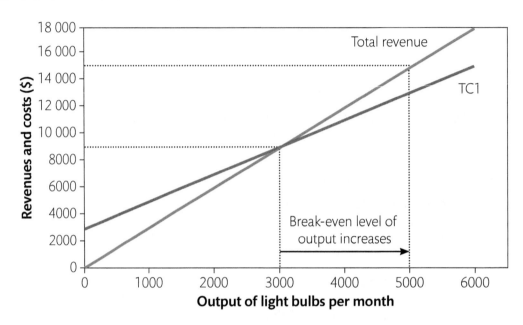

From this, a business owner can calculate the margin of safety, which is:

Actual level of output – the break-even level of output

The margin of safety is where a business is likely to make a profit.

Worked example

What is meant by 'margin of safety'? (2)

> The margin of safety is the difference between the actual level and the break-even level of output.

Using break-even analysis to help make decisions

Break-even analysis is a business planning tool. This can help a business to make decisions based on predictions of what would happen if costs change. Costs that can change are:

- fixed costs
- variable costs.

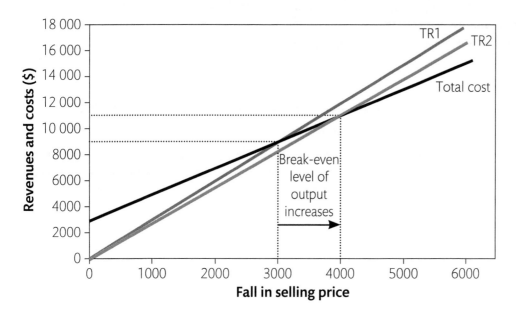

The limitations of break-even analysis

Break-even analysis only predicts what *might* happen, not what *will* happen.

Figure 4.7 shows some other key limitations that business owners must be aware of.

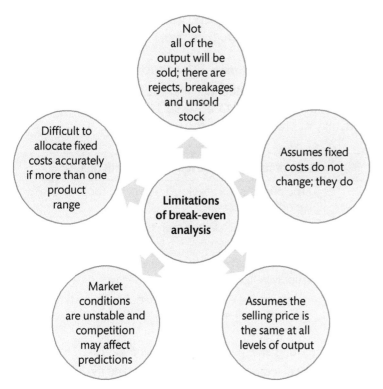

Figure 4.7 *Break-even analysis can be a useful tool, but it must be used with caution*

Review

Before you continue, make sure you are able to:

- identify and classify the different types of costs and use examples to illustrate them

- use cost data to make simple decisions

- explain, interpret and use a simple break-even chart

- understand the concept of break-even

- use a chart to make simple business decisions

- understand the limitations of break-even charts

- understand and give examples of economies and diseconomies of scale.

You need to know:
- why quality is important
- how quality production may be achieved.

Exam tip

A product or service does not need to be expensive to be good or high quality.

4.3.1 Why quality is important and how quality production might be achieved

Customers expect a product to fulfill the marketing claims made about it. If a product or service does not meet customer expectations, then it is not considered a quality good or service.

Defining quality and its importance

Quality does not mean a high price or reputation; quality means a good that is fit for purpose and meets customers' expectations.

If a customer is satisfied with the product purchased, the business will achieve the following benefits:

- positive reputation
- repeat custom
- fewer returned goods.

A low-priced good can be considered high quality if the product fulfills the expectations of the customer. A high-priced good can be considered low quality if it does not meet customer requirements.

The benefits of improving the quality of products and processes

As businesses often operate in competitive markets, they have to ensure that customer expectations are met. One way of ensuring this happens is by improving the quality of products and processes.

Exam tip

While improving quality may be expensive, it decreases mistakes, faults and wastage, which increases profits.

Benefits of investing in and improving quality	Costs of failing to invest in or maintain quality
✓ It helps to create or maintain a good reputation for the business.	✗ The business will develop a reputation for poor quality goods or services.
✓ It helps to create or reinforce a strong brand image.	✗ Customers will tell their friends and family members not to use the business.
✓ Customers will share their positive experiences with friends and family, or with other consumers via social media or on internet sites such as Trip Advisor for hotels and holidays and Zagat for restaurant reviews.	✗ Sales and market share will be lost to rival firms able to supply better quality goods and services.
✓ It helps the business gain a competitive advantage over rival firms which, in turn, will increase its sales and market share.	✗ Costs will increase because the business needs to devote more staff to handling refunds and responding to complaints.
✓ It helps to build and maintain customer loyalty and repeat custom.	✗ Profits and the value of the business are likely to fall.
✓ Long-term profitability is likely to increase.	✗ Staff turnover is likely to be higher and the business will not be able to attract high-quality managers and employees because of its poor reputation.
✓ The business can attract and retain skilled staff because of its good reputation and increasing profitability.	

There are different levels of managing and improving quality:

Quality control

This involves inspecting products and removing items with faults or defects before goods are shipped to retailers or customers.

Quality control specialists or inspectors perform this function. This does not stop errors from happening but ensures the reputation of the business is upheld and minimizes the cost of providing replacement goods.

Advantages	Disadvantages
✓ It ensures faulty items are removed from sale before they are sold or delivered to customers. ✓ Production workers do not require additional training. ✓ If possible, materials and component parts from faulty items can be recovered and reused.	✗ It does not fix the reason why product defects or errors occur during production. ✗ Materials and component parts may be wasted if it is not possible to recover them from faulty items. ✗ Additional items may be required to be made to replace the faulty ones. ✗ Additional resources, including materials, staff time, equipment use and power, will be used up making the additional items. ✗ It is not an effective way of controlling the quality of services: a poor service will only be discovered after it has been delivered to a customer and a complaint has been received.

Quality assurance

This involves setting and monitoring quality standards at all stages of the production process to reduce the chance of errors and defects.

Quality assurance aims to reduce the chance of defects before they occur, which saves money and the business's reputation. Often called **total quality management (TQM)**, it aims to achieve zero defects through continuous improvements by utilizing the '**right first time**' process. This increases efficiency and reduces lead time, waste and costs.

See page 116 for advantages and disadvantages of quality assurance.

Advantages	Disadvantages
✓ The risk of defects and errors occurring is reduced.	✗ It is more difficult to implement across an organization than quality control inspections because it relies on all employees observing and meeting quality standards.
✓ Waste is reduced as fewer items have to be scrapped or reworked.	✗ More employee training is required in how to identify and correct defects or errors.
✓ Customer complaints are reduced.	✗ Some defects and errors may still occur.

Apply

Identify as many quality marks and standards in your country as you can. Test your friends on what they represent.

Figure 4.8 *Some examples of quality marks and standards*

Quality marks and standards

If businesses are able to demonstrate high levels of quality, they can apply for and display quality marks (see Figure 4.8) on their goods.

Some advantages of quality marks are:

- increased customer confidence
- competitive advantage
- free or low-cost marketing tool
- they can attract customers away from competitors.

Worked example

Do you think that effective quality control is enough for a factory? Justify your answer. (6)

Quality control means testing the quality of the goods and services once they have been produced. If the factory stops a faulty good from reaching their customer, then they will have less goods returned and will maintain their reputation for high-quality goods, but they will not be solving the problem of making defective goods. Therefore, effective quality control is not enough, and the business should invest in quality assurance procedures which will stop mistakes before they happen and reduce the number of defective goods produced.

Review

Before you continue, make sure you are able to explain:

- the meaning and importance of quality
- how quality may be achieved
- the concept of quality control
- the concept of quality assurance.

You need to know the main factors influencing:

- the location decisions of a business
- the relocation decisions of a business.

4.4.1 The main factors influencing the location and relocation decisions of a business

When businesses are created, the location must be chosen carefully. Most location decisions aim to:

- minimize costs of production
- maximize potential advantages.

Location decisions

Factors that affect location decisions are shown in Figure 4.9.

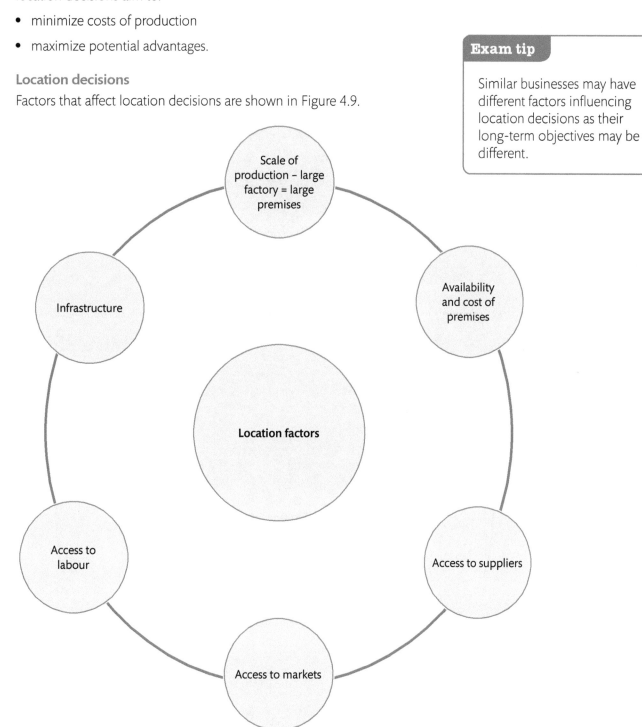

Figure 4.9 *A business or organization must locate their premises strategically*

Worked example

Identify and explain two possible advantages for a business of locating their new factory close to suppliers of their raw materials. (6)

> One advantage is that transport costs will be lower. The lower costs will maximize the profits. Another advantage is that the business will be able to use the just-in-time method. This will reduce the need for storage, so the business can buy a smaller factory, saving fixed costs.

Globalization

As businesses grow, there are opportunities for them to relocate to other countries. This is a part of what is known as **globalization**.

Globalization occurs due to:

- developing economies
- improvements in global transport and communications
- increased international trade.

Factors that influence globalization decisions are shown in Figure 4.10.

Exam tip

A decision to relocate overseas to minimize costs may affect customer perception of the brand and affect sales.

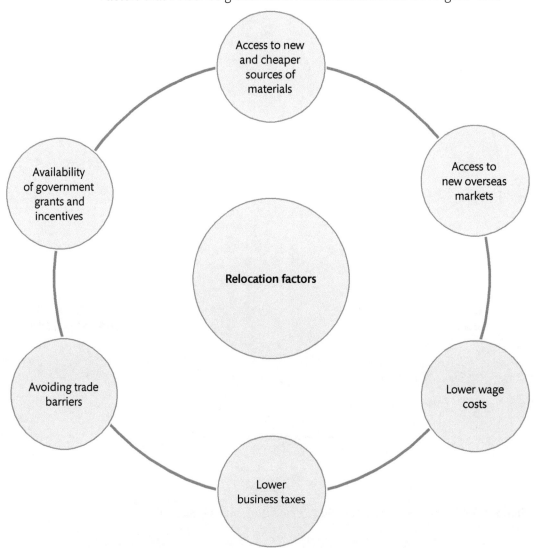

Figure 4.10 *There are various push and pull factors that cause a business to relocate*

Legal controls

When businesses expand both in their home country and overseas, they must be aware of any legal controls that can influence and restrict location decisions.

Governments may protect certain areas and existing businesses from uncontrolled growth, and encourage expansion where business activity adds to jobs, income and increased social welfare.

Ways that governments may influence growth include:

- **Planning laws** – may protect certain areas and create restrictions on the types of businesses that can set up new premises, such as:

  o   protection of local and natural environment

  o   noise and traffic restrictions

  o   historical and cultural restrictions.

- **Building regulations** – standards of construction are important when constructing buildings. Standards include:

  o   structural

  o   fire and safety

  o   energy efficiency.

There are also restrictions based on the local environment. These all may add significant costs to locating a business in certain areas.

 Apply

Select a business activity that you would like to start when you are older. Where would you locate your premises? Try to justify your choice.

Review

Before you continue, make sure you are able to:

- identify the main factors influencing location and relocation decisions

- explain factors relevant to manufacturing and service businesses

- recommend and justify an appropriate location for a business in a given circumstance.

Exam tip

Some questions require you to use evidence and information from the text above them for you to achieve full marks. If the question refers to the text, then you must too.

Exam-style questions

Unit 4

Sally owns a small factory batch producing sweatshirts for local shops to sell to tourists. As the market is seasonal, Sally knows she must budget carefully to make sure she can cover her costs all year round. As her break-even point is high, Sally is considering buying new machinery which will replace some of her labour force. This machine will be able to increase her output by 30 per cent.

(a) What is meant by 'batch production'? (2)

(b) Identify two fixed costs for a factory. (2)

(c) What is meant by the term 'seasonal'? (2)

(d) Explain the term 'budgeting'. (2)

(e) Explain the term 'break-even point'. (2)

(f) Identify and explain two factors that will affect a decision to invest in new machinery. (4)

(g) Identify and explain two potential reasons why Sally's break-even point is high. (4)

(h) Identify and explain two advantages of quality control for Sally's factory. (6)

(i) Do you think Sally should buy the new machinery? Justify your answer. (6)

Unit 5:
Financial information and decisions

Unit outline

While it is important to have excellent operations management to manage the decisions regarding production and production methods, it is also important to ensure that the business is able to make a profit and carry on trading.

A business must therefore be aware of its financial position by gathering and analysing the **financial information and decisions** made to ensure the business is able to carry on trading profitably.

Your revision checklist

Either tick these boxes to build a record of your revision, **or** use them to identify your strengths and weaknesses.

Specification	Theme	☺	☺	☹
5.1 Business finance: needs and sources	5.1.1 The need for business finance			
	5.1.2 The main sources of business finance			
5.2 Cash flow forecasting and working capital	5.2.1 Cash			
	5.2.2 Working capital			
5.3 Income statements	5.3.1 Profit and its importance			
	5.3.2 Income statements			
5.4 Statements of financial position	5.4.1 The main elements of a statement of financial position			
	5.4.2 How to interpret a simple statement of financial position			
5.5 Analysis of accounts	5.5.1 Profitability			
	5.5.2 Liquidity			
	5.5.3 Why and how accounts are used			

You need to know:

- the need for business finance
- the main sources of business finance.

5.1.1 The need for business finance

Capital

 Recap

All businesses and organizations need capital (finance) to start up and continue their business activities. If a business does not have enough capital to invest, it will struggle to set up and will fail before it starts.

Exam tip

Capital refers to the money used to invest into business assets.

Capital expenditure is used on non-current assets, while revenue expenditure is used for current assets.

Capital can be classified into three different areas:

1. **Venture** (used to start business opportunities) which is invested from loans, savings or investors.

2. **Fixed** (used for non-current assets) which is not meant to be sold for a profit.

3. **Working** (used for current assets) which is meant to finance day-to-day operations and running costs.

Business start-ups need capital for:

- the purchase or hire of fixed assets such as premises and equipment
- the purchase of materials
- the payment of any business fees and licences.

Business expansion needs capital to:

- fund the research and development of new products
- replace old equipment and machinery with new technology
- set up overseas operations
- take over another company.

Business survival requires capital to:

- cover any losses
- continue to pay short-term expenses such as wages, electricity and telephone bills, which are necessary to continue in business.

Businesses need capital to fund two main forms of expenditure.

- **Capital expenditure** is money spent on acquiring long-lived assets (or non-current assets) such as premises, vehicles and equipment.
- **Revenue expenditure** is money spent on running costs including wages, rent, telephone charges and other overheads.

Capital is often classified according to how it is used in business.

- **Venture capital** is often used to describe funds available for businesses to start up and for small businesses with exceptional growth and profit potential.
- **Fixed capital** is invested in long-lived, non-current assets.
- **Working capital** is used to finance day-to-day operations or running costs.

Short and long-term finance

A business which needs short-term finance will use different types of finance to a business that needs long-term finance.

Short-term finance	Long-term finance
Usually to be paid back within one year	Will usually take more than a year to pay back
Used to pay for small items which are replaced frequently	Used to pay for machinery with a long productive life and often paid back in regular instalments
May be used for short-term revenue expenditures (quarterly or annual bills or bulk purchases)	Repaid with output produced by the long-term asset

 Worked example

What is meant by 'short-term finance'? (2)

> Short-term finance is meant to be paid back within one year and is used for short-term expenditure like raw materials.

5.1.2 The main sources of business finance

Internal sources of finance

The main methods of internal finance are:

Retained profits: capital saved for future use and not paid out to shareholders.

Advantages of using retained profits	Disadvantages of using retained profits
✓ Profits do not have to be repaid. ✓ There are no interest charges to pay. ✓ Profits can be used to expand the business and increase future profitability.	✗ New and small businesses may have very little or no profit to draw on. ✗ Retaining profits to buy assets reduces dividend payments to business owners.

Personal savings: owners' investment, often used by sole traders and partnerships.

Advantages of using owners' savings	Disadvantages of using owners' savings
✓ They do not have to be repaid. ✓ There are no interest charges to pay. ✓ They are available to use quickly.	✗ Small business owners may have few savings to draw on. ✗ Using their own savings increases the financial risk taken by owners.

 Recap

Internal finance is defined as raising capital from a business's own sources. External finance is defined as raising finance from organizations that are not part of the business.

Exam tip

When exam questions ask for suitable sources of finance, make sure you do not use long-term sources of finances for short-term expenditure.

Selling off **assets**: surplus, unwanted or obsolete equipment, unsold products and unused materials.

Advantages of selling assets	Disadvantages of selling assets
✓ It is an easy and cheap way to raise finance.	✗ Small businesses may have few or no surplus assets to sell.
✓ Selling off stocks reduces storage requirements.	✗ It may take time to find willing buyers.

Sale and **lease back**: raising immediate capital from non-current assets such as land, machinery and buildings, then renting them back for an agreed fee.

Advantages of sale and lease back	Disadvantages of sale and lease back
✓ It provides cash for investments in other productive assets.	✗ Monthly or annual lease payments can be expensive.
✓ The seller retains control of the productive assets.	✗ The business needs to find a leasing company that will agree to buy the assets.

External sources of finance

There are two types of external finance:

1. **Debt** – a repayable loan often from money lending institutions.

2. **Equity** – non-repayable investment in a limited company by shareholders.

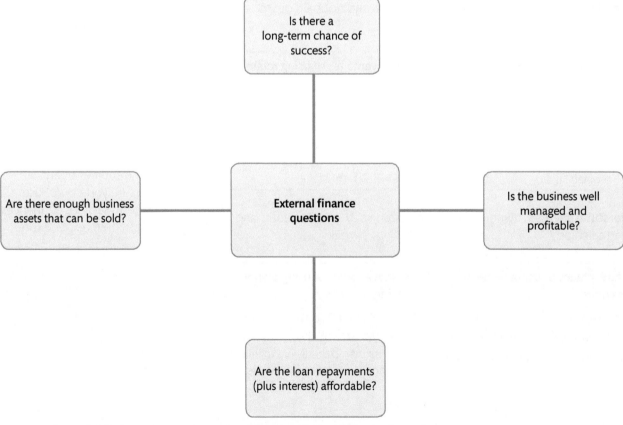

Figure 5.1 *Before an external provider of finance will provide funds, they will ask a number of questions*

External providers of finance include those shown in Figure 5.2.

> ### Exam tip
>
> A business will approach different types of external finance providers due to factors including size of business, amount of capital requested and credit history.

Short-term finance options

Trade credit: Short-term finance available from suppliers of current assets, e.g. buy now, pay later. Payment is made once finished goods are sold and helps to manage cash flow.

Hire purchase (HP) and leasing: Allows a business to rent high-value, long-term assets for a monthly fee, including interest. A business that uses HP will own the asset once the last payment has been made (but not before). A business that uses leasing will return the asset once the contract has expired.

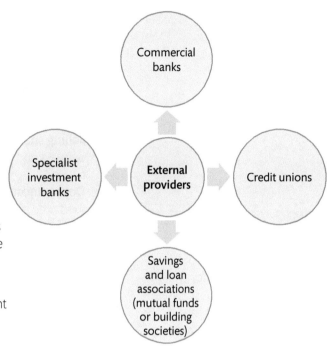

Figure 5.2 *A range of potential sources of external finance exist, each with its own set of risks and rewards*

Short-term finance	Advantages	Disadvantages
An **overdraft** allows a business customer to "overdraw" their bank account by an agreed amount. It provides a convenient short-term loan, for example, to pay a large electricity or wage bill.	✓ This is a quick and easy method of borrowing a limited amount of money for a short period of time.	✗ **Interest rates** or charges can be high, often much higher than a bank loan and can vary over time. ✗ An overdraft can be withdrawn at any time requiring the borrower to repay it in full.
A **credit card** can be used to make purchases of supplies, travel and equipment. Payment is not required until a month or so later. Interest is charged if the full balance is not paid off within this time.	✓ Using a credit card is a quick and easy way of borrowing money for a short period of time. ✓ There is an interest-free period, often up to 56 days.	✗ Interest rates or charges vary but can be very high. ✗ The amount a business can borrow is limited.

Long-term debt finance options

Long-term finance	Advantages	Disadvantages
A **commercial loan** is normally used to finance capital expenditures. Repayment periods can vary from 6–12 months to 15 or more years.	✓ A commercial loan is relatively easy to arrange. ✓ There is a choice of repayment periods. ✓ Large profitable companies may get preferential interest rates on large loans.	✗ Monthly repayments must be made inclusive of interest or fees. ✗ Interest rates or charges are normally fixed for the length of the loan and can be high. This helps reduce uncertainty. ✗ Security or **collateral** is required.
A **mortgage** is a long-term loan, usually repayable over 25 or 30 years, for the purchase of property. Commercial mortgages are used to finance the purchase or construction of business premises.	✓ There is a choice of repayment periods. ✓ Large profitable companies may receive preferential interest rates on large loans.	✗ Interest rates or charges may be fixed or variable but can be high. ✗ There may be an arrangement fee and a large deposit may be required. ✗ The loan will be secured against the property. It will be sold if the business is unable to repay its loan.

Long-term equity finance options

Equity financing is the process of generating capital by selling shares in a business, creating new or additional shareholders.

- **Venture capital:** Organizations that invest funds into new and innovative businesses with high growth and profit potential. Often share in the ownership and management of the new businesses.
- **Selling shares:** Investors who invest capital become shareholders in the business and, in return, receive dividends. The original investment is never repaid.
- **Debentures:** Long-term loan certificates issued by limited companies for a fixed time period, which are then repaid in full with interest at the end of the term.

> ### Exam tip
>
> Business angels are only a source of finance for small- to medium-size businesses – they do not invest into established businesses.

Advantages	Disadvantages
✓ Share issues can raise significant new capital. ✓ They provide permanent capital because the capital never has to be repaid by the company.	✗ Issuing shares is complex and expensive. ✗ Issuing more shares can reduce the market price of existing shares. ✗ The original owners of a company may lose control as more shares are issued.

State finance options

State finance can be provided to start-up businesses that can help create employment and income. It is often available in areas of high unemployment or when research and development is needed in new industries.

Advantages	Disadvantages
✓ Grants and concessions are non-repayable. ✓ Governments may provide finance and low-interest loans when banks refuse to do so.	✗ A government may insist on certain conditions, such as creating or maintaining an agreed number of jobs in a specified location.

Alternative sources of finance

Many people who own few assets are unable to access loans and funding from regular sources. Developing economies often have high levels of poverty and lending is very difficult. Specialist providers of **microfinance** have grown to fill this undeveloped market.

Crowd funding: Borrowing small amounts of capital from large numbers of investors. This is either an equity or reward-based investment accessed through the internet.

Figure 5.3 *Microfinance is a relatively new form of business funding, and is designed to help lift individuals and communities out of poverty*

Worked example

Identify two methods of short-term financing that could be used for purchasing raw materials. (2)

Overdraft, trade credit.

Choosing a method of finance

Figure 5.4 *Managers and owners must assess the costs and benefits of different options*

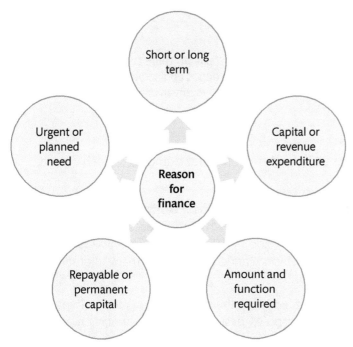

Figure 5.5 *Businesses may need additional financing for a variety of reasons*

 Apply

A family friend is thinking about setting up a business selling mobile phones, and you must advise them on the most suitable types of finance available to them. Create a two-page leaflet advising on the short- and long-term options.

 Review

Before you continue, make sure you are able to:

- identify the main needs for business finance including start-up capital, fixed and working capital

- understand the difference between short- and long-term finance needs

- identify the main internal and external sources of capital

- explain the difference between long- and short-term needs and options

- explain the main factors to consider when making financial choices

- recommend and justify appropriate sources of finance.

You need to know:
- the importance of cash and cash flow forecasting
- working capital.

 Recap

Successful businesses must manage their cash flow to make sure that there are enough liquid assets available to pay the daily running costs.

5.2.1 Cash

The importance of cash

If a business cannot pay its wages or bills, employees will not come to work and suppliers will not provide resources. The business will fail as it has a cash flow problem.

A business must balance its cash inflows and cash outflows.

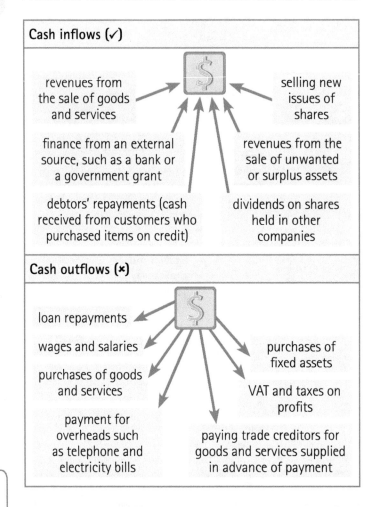

Cash flow

A business must hold and forecast the amount of **cash** it needs.

Exam tip

Remember, cash is the most liquid current asset: the other three are debtors, cash-in-bank and stock.

 Apply

Calculate your working capital by assessing your own assets and liabilities. Can you think of any ways to improve your liquidity?

Escada was once a leading fashion clothing company. It started as a small partnership in Munich in 1978, became a publicly traded company in 1986, and by 1990 it had grown into one of the world's best-known fashion brands, popular with many international film stars and celebrities.

However, in recent years the company struggled with internal management disputes, design flops and a shrinking market for luxury fashion items. The company had a string of retail outlets all over the world and a number of these had proved unpopular.

It had also invested heavily in developing new summer and winter collections that proved to be unpopular. Stocks of the clothes built up as sales fell sharply and the company plunged into loss. Unable to sell off its stocks of unwanted clothing, cash flows into the business were not sufficient to cover running costs and, importantly, were not enough to pay for the design, development and launch of a new clothing collection for the next year.

With no way to launch a new collection that may have helped boost sales, and with losses mounting, investors lost confidence in the company and its share price plummeted on the stock market. Creditors were unwilling to lend more to the company and so it became insolvent and was declared bankrupt.

Although Escada was once a very profitable business, it quickly ran out of cash because it had expanded too quickly, had tied up too much cash in stocks of clothing that proved unpopular with consumers and was unable to persuade creditors to lend it more money to help pays its bills.

Many cash outflows are regular monthly, quarterly or annual payments that can be planned for.

Infrequent or unexpected bills cannot be accurately planned for. This means a cash reserve must be held for unplanned needs.

A business should always aim for a cash **surplus** at the end of every week, month or accounting period. This will then cover any times when there is a cash **deficit**.

 Worked example

> Identify and explain two advantages of cash flow forecasting. (4)
>
> > The business will always have enough cash to buy its stock, which means it will not need to take an expensive short-term loan to buy the raw materials needed. The business will be able to afford the repayments for new machinery, which means they will be able to keep producing and earning revenue.

Cash flow forecasting

If a business does not accurately predict the amount of cash needed, it cannot pay its bills. A business then has limited options:

- selling assets quickly to raise short-term capital which may harm productivity
- borrowing money at high interest rates, which may reduce profitability.

A business mush create **cash flow forecasts**. These may be based on:

- historical data
- predictions based on anticipated orders.

A cash flow forecast (as on page 130) will predict monthly cash in and outflow and calculate expected cash balances every month. This will aid in the budgeting of a business.

A cash flow forecast (as on page 130)

Exam tip

A business can have too much cash. This means that money is not invested into production and may be reducing revenue.

$		January	February	March	April	May	June
Opening balance (A)		0	$3000	–$7000	–$10000	–$5500	0
Cash inflows							
Cash sales					$18000	$18000	$18000
Credit sales				$10000			
New capital	Bank loan	$6500					
	Savings	$4000					
Total cash inflows (B)		$10500	0	$10000	$18000	$18000	$18000
Cash outflows							
Wages and salaries			$6500	$7000	$8000	$8000	$8000
Cash purchases	Equipment	$5000					
	Materials		$2000	$3000	$3000	$3000	$3000
Overheads	Loan repayments		$1000	$1000	$1000	$1000	$1000
	Rent	$500	$500	$500	$500	$500	$500
	Electricity			$1000			$1200
	Lease charges	$800			$800		
	Insurance	$1200					
	Telephone			$400			$300
	Maintenance						
	Other			$100	$200		
Total cash outflows (C)		$7500	$10000	$13000	$13500	$12500	$14000
Net cash flow (D) (= B – C)		$3000	$10000	$3000	$4500	$5500	$4000
Closing balance (= A + D)		$3000	$7000	$10000	$5500	0	$4000

Cash flow management

Profitable businesses may run short of liquid cash and have cash flow difficulties if one or more of the following problems occur:

- **holding excess inventories** – materials and finished goods mean cash is illiquid and may be difficult to sell at full price

- **expanding too quickly** – increased production requires investment before any returns are made to bolster cash reserves

- **overinvesting in non-current assets** – buying expensive machinery may reduce working capital – leasing or HP may be more suitable

- **borrowing too much** – interest payments may mean profit margins are too small

- **poor credit control** – allowing unreliable or poor paying customers to have too much credit

- **inflation** – may impact upon the revenue and costs if poorly managed

- **seasonal variation** – unseasonable weather may unexpectedly reduce or increase demand for a particular product out of the regular peak or slow periods.

All of these options have associated costs and businesses must ensure all effects are minimized.

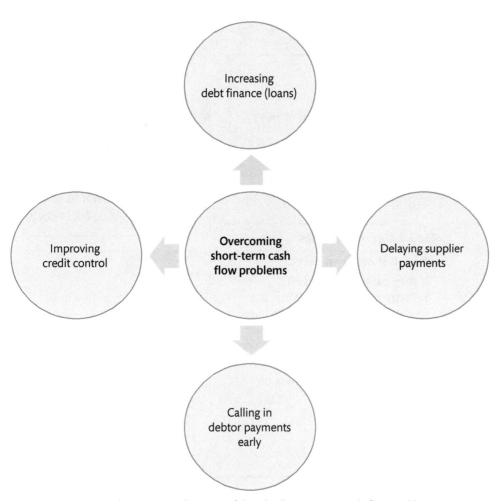

Figure 5.6 *A business may be successful and still experience cash flow problems*

5.2.2 Working capital

The importance of working capital

A business must avoid continuous short-term cash flow problems by managing cash flow effectively and having a positive working capital.

This will avoid running out of cash, especially if there are unforeseen costs. Stakeholders are able to measure the viability of a business by assessing cash flow.

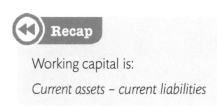

Working capital is:

Current assets – current liabilities

Figure 5.7 *Current assets > Current liabilities*

Worked example

What is meant by 'working capital'? (2)

> Working capital is cash available to spend and is calculated by subtracting current liabilities from current assets.

Methods of ensuring a positive cash flow

Increase current assets	Reduce current liabilities
✓ **Improve cash inflows**, for example, by offering customers price discounts. This can help boost demand and sales revenues.	✓ **Pay off short-term debts.**
	✓ **If they cannot be paid off, refinance short-term debts** with long-term loans. This will help lower the cost of monthly repayments by spreading them over a longer period of time.
✓ **Cut costs and cash outflows**, for example, by finding cheaper suppliers.	
✓ **Sell off unwanted assets** for cash.	
✓ **Improve credit control**, to increase "good" debtors and reduce bad debts.	✓ **Reduce purchases of goods on credit**, for example, by running down excess inventories.

Figure 5.8 *How to improve the working capital position of a business*

Exam tip

Negative **working capital** is when short-term debts exceed the value of current assets and a business does not have the funds available to cover costs.

Exam tip

If a business is at the beginning of its life cycle, it may be difficult to have positive cash flow. This does not mean poor cash flow as long as the deficit has been planned for.

 Review

Before you continue, make sure you are able to:

- understand the concept and importance of cash flow and cash flow forecasting for a business
- explain why cash is important for a business
- explain the elements of a cash flow forecast
- amend, interpret and explain the importance of a cash flow forecast
- explain how short-term cash flow problems may be overcome.

You need to know:

- what profit is and why it is important
- income statements.

5.3.1 Profit and its importance

How a profit is made

Profit is generated by having revenue which is larger than costs. If costs are higher than revenue, a business makes a **loss**.

Costs depend on the type of business, but generally include:

- staff wages
- raw materials
- overheads (fixed costs).

Businesses can earn income from non-trading activities such as:

- interest on savings
- rent from unused premises
- brand license payments.

Profit = gross profit + non-trading income

The importance of making a profit

Profit is one of the main rewards for enterprising and risk taking in business. It can be used for either shareholder funds or as a source of finance for investment. Without profit, business owners will not be able to pay themselves a wage or be able to invest in the future.

Without the hope of a reward, most people would be unwilling to start their own businesses. A person with the capital available to start their own business has three choices:

- spend money on wants and needs
- save the money in the bank
- invest the money into a business opportunity.

Each option has its own risks and rewards. The higher the risk, the higher the reward that is needed.

 Worked example

> Identify two factors that may affect the profit of a business. (2)
>
> Increased cost of raw materials; a falling selling price.

Profit is a measure of success. If a business has been successful, this information can be used as:

- evidence for a bank loan or other borrowing methods
- evidence for rewards for employees and shareholders
- a way of calculating corporation (government) tax
- a method of deciding where and when to invest more capital for future business opportunities.

Recap

Profit is made by risking your capital investment in the hope of making a return larger than costs.

Exam tip

Risk is necessary for business, as long as it is managed; the reward for success has to be suitable and the price of failure manageable.

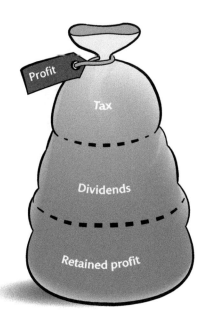

Exam tip

Be careful not to confuse cash with profit. Cash means the money a business is able to spend, while profit may be based on credit and therefore cannot be spent, creating a cash flow problem.

⏪ Recap

Income statements are used to calculate, report and monitor revenues, costs and profits of a business and last for an accounting year.

Business or company name

End of the accounting year or period covered by the income statement

Accounting for profit

Profit and loss must be accurately calculated and monitored by business owners. Records must be kept of all transactions (costs and revenues).

Profit = total revenues – total costs

5.3.2 Income statements

There are two parts to an **income statement**:

1. **The trading account**

    This calculates and records:

    - total revenue from sales
    - total cost of goods sold
    - the gross profit or loss.

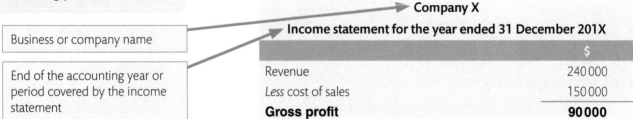

Company X
Income statement for the year ended 31 December 201X

	$
Revenue	240 000
Less cost of sales	150 000
Gross profit	**90 000**

2. **The profit and loss account**

    This calculates and records:

    - total expenses
    - profit or loss after all costs are deducted.

Total income is the same as total revenue from sales for most businesses

Total cost of the business is its cost of sales plus all other expenses

Total expenses (or fixed costs) of the business

Profit before tax = total income – total costs

The final section of the statement reports how profit after tax has been used

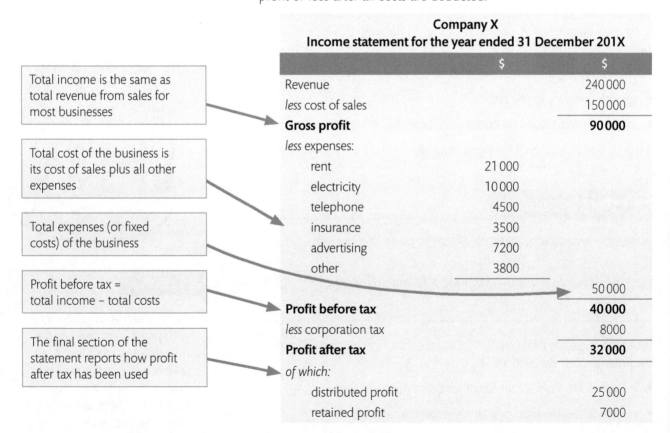

Company X
Income statement for the year ended 31 December 201X

	$	$
Revenue		240 000
less cost of sales		150 000
Gross profit		**90 000**
less expenses:		
rent	21 000	
electricity	10 000	
telephone	4500	
insurance	3500	
advertising	7200	
other	3800	
		50 000
Profit before tax		**40 000**
less corporation tax		8000
Profit after tax		**32 000**
of which:		
distributed profit		25 000
retained profit		7000

This shows whether or not a business can control costs.

Worked example

Using the income statement on page 134 calculate:

(a) gross profit

(b) profit after tax

(a) *Gross profit = revenue ($240,000) − costs (150,000) = $90,000*

(b) *Profit after tax = profit before tax ($40,000) − corporation tax ($8,000) = $32,000*

Using income statements to inform business decisions

Income statements are used by business owners and managers to:

- compare whether business profit has risen or fallen in comparison to previous years
- compare whether profit has matched market trends
- establish how much capital is available for shareholder funds or reinvestment
- compare profit with competitors (if data is available) to gauge market share or growth.

This data can then be used to project revenues and costs for future years, to make decisions on the kinds of issues shown in Figure 5.9.

> **Exam tip**
>
> A business should not only use financial indicators to make decisions, as there could be other non-financial influencing factors.
>
> A business can also choose how decisions can influence profit, and the likely outcomes.

Figure 5.9 *Income statement data can be used to inform various business decisions*

To increase gross profit	To increase profit (or reduce loss)
✓ Increase total sales, for example, by introducing a new product, expanding overseas or increasing advertising – but will this be cost-effective and raise revenue by more than it adds to total costs? ✓ Raise the selling price to increase the revenue per item sold – but how competitive is the market for the product? If demand is price elastic, total sales and revenue will fall. Cutting price instead may therefore increase total sales. ✓ Reduce the cost of sales, for example, purchase items from cheaper suppliers – but are these suppliers reliable and will the quality of the items be the same?	✓ Increase gross profit. ✓ Increase non-trading income, for example, by subletting surplus space in the premises. ✓ Cut the number of office and sales staff – but staff may object and cause disruption, there may be redundancy costs and if too many employees are cut, it may reduce the ability of the business to function effectively and make sales. ✓ Find cheaper premises – but will the location be as near to customers (or major suppliers) and as profitable as the previous one? ✓ Find cheaper suppliers of electricity, insurance, maintenance and other expense items.

 Review

Before you continue, make sure you are able to:

- explain what profit is, how it is made and its importance

- the difference between profit and cash

- understand the main features of an income statement

- use simple income statements for profit-based decision making.

You need to know:
- the main elements of a statement of financial position
- how to interpret a simple statement of financial position and make deductions from it.

5.4.1 The main elements of a statement of financial position

A **statement of financial position** is out of date the moment after it is produced and can easily be manipulated by selling stock or machinery or buying new raw materials.

It deals with the finances of a business, not profit or loss or profitability.

A statement of financial position records the following elements:

ASSETS	• Items of value owned by the business
LIABILITIES	• Amount of money owed to external creditors
CAPITAL	• Amount of money invested in the business

Recap

A statement of financial position records how much a business owns and owes at the end of a 12-month accounting period.

Exam tip

A statement of financial position is like a camera snapshot – it tells you what the financial position at that particular time is, but it is easily manipulate. Smile for the camera!

Total assets = Non-current assets + Current assets	
Non-current assets (or fixed assets) These include machinery, equipment, vehicles, land and premises owned by a business and used in productive activity. They are physical assets that are usually kept and used by a business for more than one year. The value of non-current assets fall over time as they age and wear out through repeated use.	
Current assets These include cash, inventories of materials and finished products and money owed to the business by its credit customers (its **debtors** or **accounts receivable**). They are used up by a business within the next 12-month accounting period to pay its immediate debts and running costs.	

Total liabilities = Non-current liabilities + Current liabilities	
Non-current liabilities (or long-term liabilities)	**Current liabilities**
Money owed to external providers of long-term finance that are repayable over more than one year, for example, a ten-year bank loan.	Money owed to external providers of short-term finance that will fall due for repayment within 12 months, for example, a bank overdraft.
Bank loan Mortgage Debenture	Trade credit Overdraft Credit card

Exam tip

Assets = liabilities + owners capital

Recap

A statement of financial position shows how capital has been invested in a business and how it has been financed.

Worked example

Identify two non-current assets of the business in Figure 5.10, and name two ways investments can be funded.

Two non-current assets are machinery and equipment. Money invested can be funded by owners' capital (equity), provided by owners or shareholders, or liabilities, e.g. loans and other repayable debts.

5.4.2 How to interpret a simple statement of financial position

Business or company name, plus date of balance sheet

Final column is used to total the amounts entered in previous columns

Nice Creams Balance sheet at 30 June last year			$	$
		Machinery	75 000	
		Equipment	30 000	
		Vehicles	25 000	
①	A	**Non-current assets**		130 000
		Cash	15 000	
		Inventories	21 000	
		Accounts receivable	14 000	
②	B	**Current assets**		50 000
③	C	**Total assets (A + B)**		180 000
		Accounts payable	9 000	
		Bank overdraft	1 000	
④	D	**Current liabilities**		10 000
		Bank loan	60 000	
⑤	E	**Non-current liabilities**		60 000
⑥	F	**Total assets less total liabilities (C – D – E)**		110 000
		Shareholders' funds		
⑦	G	Share capital	78 000	
	H	Retained profits	32 000	
⑧	I	**Total shareholders' funds (G + H) = (F)**		110 000

Figure 5.10 *Balance sheet (full format)*

① The total value of the **non-current assets** of the company at the date given on the balance sheet.

② The total **current assets** of the company, including amounts owed to it by customers who have been sold goods on credit. They are its **debtors** or **accounts receivable**.

③ The **total assets** of the company: **Non-current assets + Current assets**

④ The total **current liabilities** of the company: the short-term debts of the business which must be repaid within 12 months. They include bank overdrafts and amounts due to suppliers for items purchased by the business on credit. These suppliers are its **creditors** but in a balance sheet they are recorded as **accounts payable**.

⑤ The long-term loan capital or **non-current liabilities** of the company. These are bank loans and other debts that the company will repay over more than one year.

⑥ The value of **total assets – total liabilities**. This shows how much capital would remain invested in the company after it had paid off all its liabilities. The amount of capital remaining would belong to the shareholders.

⑦ This section is used to record the total funds or capital invested in the company by its shareholders. It consists of:

⑧ • **share capital**: the amount of capital originally invested by the shareholders when they purchased new shares issued by the company
• **retained profits**: profits accumulated by the company from the current and previous years that were not distributed to the shareholders.

Shareholders investing into a limited company have their investment labelled as shareholders' funds. This is important to shareholders, as it shows the actual worth of their investment into the organization.

In an exam, a summary of the full statement will be shown, which shows more clearly how the company assets are financed.

Exam tip

Total assets = total liabilities + shareholders funds

	Nice Creams Summary of balance sheet at 30 June last year		
		$	$
A	**Non-current assets**		**130 000**
B	Current assets	50 000	
D	Current liabilities	10 000	
WC	**Working capital (B − D)**		**40 000**
NA	**Total assets − current liabilities (A + WC)**		**170 000**
	Financed by		
E	Non-current liabilities	60 000	
I	Shareholders' funds	110 000	
CE	**Capital employed (E + I) = (NA)**		**170 000**

Figure 5.11 *Balance sheet (summary format)*

9	**Current assets − current liabilities = working capital**. This is capital available to the company to pay its ongoing running costs. It is positive because the value of its current assets is more than enough to pay off its current liabilities. No business could survive very long without sufficient working capital to pay its short-term debts. Suppliers of materials, electricity, telephone services and other creditors would stop supplying items if the business could not pay its bills.	Working capital is also known as **net current assets**.
10	**Total assets − current liabilities**. This is equal to the "fixed capital" invested in non-current assets plus the working capital of the company. It shows how much long-term capital has been invested or "employed" in assets that will allow the company to continue production and trading well into the future.	Total assets less current liabilities may also be described as **net assets** in some examination papers.
11	This section shows the sources of the long-term **capital employed** in the non-current assets and working capital of the company. It consists of: • **non-current liabilities**: the long-term liabilities or loan capital of the company • **shareholders' funds**: the permanent capital of the company raised from the sale of shares or financed from retained profits.	Capital employed is sometimes called **fixed and working capital employed**.

Worked example

Use the statement of financial position above. Do you think the business is in a strong financial position? Justify your answer. (6)

The business has five current assets as liabilities, so is able to cover all of its short-term debts easily. Fixed capital is also positive, which means it has cash available to invest into new machinery, so I think that it is in a strong financial position as it has the cash to survive and expand in the future.

Review

Before you continue, make sure you are able to:

• understand the main elements of a statement of financial position

• use examples to illustrate the main classifications of assets and liabilities

• understand and interpret a simple statement of financial position.

You need to know:
- profitability
- liquidity
- how to calculate and analyse profitability ratios and liquidity ratios
- why and how accounts are used.

 **Recap**

Profitability measures the ability of a business to generate profits.

5.5.1 Profitability

Profitability is important for the following reasons:

- the business has retained funds for investment and growth
- it is easier to attract investors if profitability is high
- the value of the business increases, which allows for a capital gain
- it allows a business to repay debts, which reduces costs and gearing.

Interpreting financial performance

Profit figures by themselves do not reveal much about the financial strength and performance of a business.

Picking one figure to judge performance can be misleading. For this reason it is important to compare two or more ratios that may provide a better picture of the business.

The three profitability ratios used to measure how well a business is using its assets to generate profits are:

1. gross profit margin (GPM)
2. profit margin
3. return on capital employed (ROCE).

Gross profit margin (GPM)

This shows how much profit a business makes when the cost of goods has been paid.

$$Gross\ profit\ margin\ (\%) = \frac{Gross\ profit}{Revenue} \times 100$$

A lower than average GPM could indicate that products are sold too cheaply.

The gross profit margin will increase if:	The gross profit margin will decrease if:
• there is an increase in sales revenue • the selling price of each item can be increased without a significant loss of sales, for example, because consumer demand is rising and there are few other businesses to compete with • early payment discounts given to credit customers (debtors) are reduced • the cost of sales falls, for example, because the business purchases items from cheaper suppliers or buys more in bulk to take advantages of discounts offered by suppliers.	• there is a fall in sales revenue • the selling price of each item is reduced, for example, because competitors have reduced their prices • the business offers more generous early payment discounts to credit customers in an attempt to boost credit sales and bring forward cash inflows • the costs of sales rises, for example, because suppliers have increased their selling prices.

Profit margin

This shows how much profit a business makes when all costs and expenses have been paid.

The profit margin indicates the efficiency of a business to convert sales into income to investors.

A higher than average profit margin indicates a low-risk, efficient and competitive business.

$$Profit\ margin\ (\%) = \frac{Profit\ before\ tax}{Revenue} \times 100$$

The profit margin will increase if:	The profit margin will decrease if:
• gross profit increases • non-trading income increases • overheads are reduced.	• gross profit falls • non-trading income falls • overheads increase.

A falling profit margin could indicate rising expenses.

Return on capital employed (ROCE)

This shows the profit of a company as a percentage of the total value of capital employed.

If the ROCE is lower than a bank savings account, then the return is not worth the risk of investing.

The ROCE allows an investor to compare the returns of different options.

$$ROCE\ (\%) = \frac{Profit\ before\ tax}{Capital\ employed} \times 100$$

The ROCE will increase if:	The ROCE will decrease if:
• profit increases • capital employed is reduced without any impact on profit • capital employed is unchanged but is used more efficiently to increase profit.	• profit falls • capital employed is increased but without any impact on profit • capital employed is unchanged but is used less efficiently so profit falls.

 Worked example

What is meant by 'return on capital employed'? (2)

ROCE is a profitability ratio which expresses the profit of a company as a percentage of the capital employed.

Exam tip

A **liquid asset** is anything that can be sold quickly and converted into cash, such as debtors and stock.

Exam tip

In the short term, cash flow and liquidity are more important than profitability, which is more important in the long term.

5.5.2 Liquidity

If a business is illiquid, there are two possible outcomes:

- it is necessary to obtain an expensive bank loan or sell important assets to raise capital quickly, which can affect profitability

- a business may be forced to close and go bankrupt if cash cannot be raised.

Liquidity ratios can act as early warning signals for financial problems due to unexpected bills or a need for cash.

Current ratio

The **Current ratio** measures the ability of a business to pay its short-term debt (current liabilities).

Current assets are usually expected to be roughly double the current liabilities. If the current ratio is lower than 2, the business could run out of liquid cash.

If the current ratio is lower than 1 then the business is insolvent and cannot pay its immediate debts.

$$Current\ ratio = \frac{current\ assets}{current\ liabilities}$$

The current ratio will increase if:	The current ratio will decrease if:
• the amount of cash the business holds on its premises or in its bank accounts is increased • current liabilities are reduced, for example, because the business pays off its creditors and bank overdraft using a long-term loan • overheads are reduced so cash outflows decrease • purchases of equipment and other non-current assets are delayed so that the business holds on to its cash for longer • the amount of profits paid out to the business owners is reduced (or dividends to shareholders are reduced) so that the business retains more profit to hold as cash.	• the amount of cash the business holds on its premises or in its bank accounts is reduced, for example, due to falling cash sales • current liabilities increase, for example, because the business increases its purchases on credit or overdraws its bank account • overheads increase so cash outflows from the business increase to pay the higher costs • cash spending on equipment and other non-current assets is increased • retained profits are reduced and paid to the business owners instead.

Acid-test ratio

The **acid-test ratio** measures the ability of a business to pay its short-term debt (current liabilities), excluding finished products and raw materials which can take longer to turn into cash.

Current assets are usually expected to be roughly equal to current liabilities. If the current ratio is lower than 1, the business could run out of liquid cash and be forced to sell raw materials and stock at a lower than expected price for a quick sale.

This may be difficult in times of economic uncertainty or low consumer demand.

$$Acid\text{-}test\ ratio = \frac{(current\ assets - inventories)}{current\ liabilities}$$

 Worked example

Identify two possible advantages of using liquidity ratios to make investment decisions. (6)

> The business will be able to decide how much cash they need to borrow to buy the machinery, which will minimize any interest payments. Also, by using the acid-test ratio, the business can see that they need to sell some of their inventory, which will reduce the risk of having to take out expensive short-term loans to pay unexpected bills.

 Apply

Create a dominoes game with the name of accounting ratios on one half and the calculation on the other.

5.5.3 Why and how accounts are used

Preparing and using financial statements

Final accounts are produced for a number of reasons:

1. **To monitor business performance** – they provide a record of how well the business has performed over the accounting year. This can be compared with other accounting years and also competitors to analyse the relative strength of the business and to improve performance.

2. **To secure and maintain short- and long-term finance** – external finance providers are often used to provide capital for investment and expansion. Any potential investor will need to ensure that the risk is sufficient to the reward and the business is able to meet both its short- and long-term commitments.

3. **To meet legal requirements** – government tax authorities need to be able to calculate and apply corporation tax and any other taxes, such as VAT and sales taxes.

 Recap

The income statements and statement of financial position are referred to as the final accounts of a business. These are produced at the end of each financial year by law.

Exam tip

You will not be expected to produce any accounts, as these are completed by qualified accountants. All you need to do is understand the headings and examples.

Users of accounts and accounting ratios

Business owners

- Is my business profitable?
- Is profitability increasing?
- How do its profit margins and return on capital employed compare with those of competing businesses?
- If profits are falling should I withdraw my capital or sell my shares and invest the money in another more profitable enterprise?
- If profits are rising should I invest more to expand the business?
- How much is my investment worth now compared to last year?

Business managers

In addition to the final accounts we will require more regular financial reports and summaries because we need up-to-date figures to control and manage the business to:

- monitor costs, revenues and working capital
- identify any actions that need to be taken in the business to control its costs and/or boost sales
- compare business performance against competitors: are profit margins and returns on capital employed better or worse than those of competitors, and how can our business become more competitive?
- set new financial performance targets.

A new investor

- Should I invest my capital in the business (for example, by joining a partnership or buying shares in a company) or invest elsewhere?
- Will the business provide a good return on my investment?
- How do its profitability ratios compare to those of other businesses? I am unlikely to invest in the business if they are lower and have no prospect of improving.
- Has the value of the business increased or decreased over time according to its balance sheets? I am unlikely to invest in the business if its value is not growing or, worse, falling.
- Does the business hold enough current assets to settle its current liabilities? I will not invest in the business if it has a significant liquidity problem and will not be able to raise enough cash to continue operating.

- Is our employer profitable?
- Have profits been rising or falling over time?
- If profits have been falling, are our jobs secure?
- If profits have been rising, can our employer afford to increase our wages and salaries and improve our working conditions – and by how much?

Employees and trade unions

- How do the profitability ratios of the business compare to our results?
- If they are better, what actions should we take to improve our own ratios? For example, should we cut prices and increase marketing to boost sales? Can we improve efficiency to cut costs?
- How much is the business worth?
- Is the financial strength of the business, and therefore its ability to compete, improving?
- Should we try to take over the business?

A competing business

- How well are all businesses performing?
- Are they creating more output, jobs and incomes?
- How much tax revenue do they owe?
- Should the government provide financial assistance to an individual business? Is it managed well and how much financial support does it really need?

Government authorities

- Should the business be allowed to buy more items on credit?
- Is the business a good credit risk?
- How much are its total current and other liabilities?
- Will it be able to settle its debts when payment is required?
- Does it have enough working capital to continue operating?

Suppliers of goods and services on credit payment terms

Figure 5.12 *How different stakeholders will examine and question the accounts of a business*

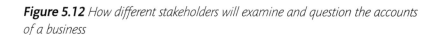

📖 **Worked example**

Identify and explain two users of published accounts. (4)

> Business owners use published accounts to see whether the business is profitable. New investors use published accounts to check if the return is suitable for the risk involved.

Limitations of accounts and accounting ratios

As all business have different requirements and the data can be manipulated easily, users have to be aware of the following limitations:

- Future performance may be different from past performance: factors including new technology, competitors and changing customer tastes may affect business.

- The impact of inflation on values: inflation can alter the real value of business assets and liabilities over time as all values are recorded as per the current price on the day of the transaction.

- Different accounting methods and years: there are different ways of valuing vehicles and non-current assets which may make it difficult to compare with other published accounts.

- Not all indicators of performance are financial: social and environmental issues are also important factors that may impact the short-term profitability and liquidity but are vital for long-term success.

Exam tip

The accounting ratios do not show what stage of the life cycle the business is operating in. A newly formed business will have different priorities to an established business.

Review

Before you continue, make sure you are able to understand:

- how to interpret financial statements by calculating and analysing accounting ratios including:
  - GPM
  - profit margin
  - ROCE
  - current ratio
  - acid-test ratio
- the concept and importance of liquidity
- how and why accounts and ratio analysis are used by different users
- how the users of accounts and ratio results may use the information to make decisions.

Exam-style questions

Unit 5

BTS uses mass production to make three different types of office chairs. Last year BTS sold 500 office chairs, although only two of the types seemed to be selling well.

After analysing the financial data shown in the table the finance director called a board meeting to discuss it.

She said: "As profitability is important, we need to do some ratio analysis to measure the business performance. In the previous year the gross profit margin was 25 per cent."

The directors are worried about rising costs but are unsure about whether to focus on quality or cost.

Revenue	$10000
Gross profit	$2000
Profit before tax	$500
Profit after tax	$250

(a) What is meant by 'ratio analysis'? (2)

(b) Identify two reasons the finance director might want to measure profitability. (2)

(c) What is meant by 'mass production'? (2)

(d) What is meant by 'profitability'? (2)

(e) Explain the term 'gross profit margin'. (2)

(f) Calculate BTS's gross profit margin for 2018 and explain the impact of the change. (4)

(g) Identify two potential stakeholders and explain why they may be interested in the accounts. (4)

(h) Identify and explain two disadvantages of BTS focusing on profit as the only target. (6)

(i) Do you think that BTS should focus on quality or cost? Justify your answer. (6)

Exam tip

Pay attention to how many examples a question is asking for. If the question asks for two, and you only provide one, you can only receive half of the available marks, even if your answer is excellent.

Unit 6:
External influences on business activity

Unit outline

A business is able to control how it produces its goods and services, which finance packages are chosen and where to be located. However, there are many influences that businesses cannot control.

A business must be aware of and consider the **external influences on business activity** to make sure that decisions take into account factors that cannot be controlled.

Your revision checklist

Either tick these boxes to build a record of your revision, **or** use them to identify your strengths and weaknesses.

Specification	Theme	☺	😐	☹
6.1: Economic issues	6.1.1 The business cycle			
	6.1.2 How control over the economy affects business activity and how business may respond			
6.2: Ethics and the environment	6.2.1 The relationship between business and the environment			
	6.2.2 Ethical issues			
6.3: Business and the international economy	6.3.1 The importance of globalization			
	6.3.2 Reasons for the importance and growth of multinational companies			
	6.3.3 The impact of exchange rates			

You need to know:
- the business cycle
- how control over the economy affects business activity and how business may respond.

6.1.1 The business cycle

Government economic objectives

The government has four main **objectives** for the national economy, as shown in Figure 6.1.

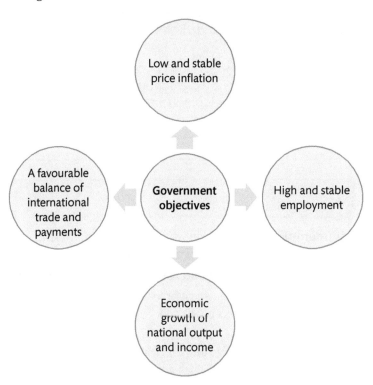

Figure 6.1 *The four objectives of any government's economic policy*

Recap

The business cycle refers to the recurring pattern of growth and decline in business activity observed in an economy over a period of time. Governments may try to control the business cycle depending on their current economic objectives.

Exam tip

The objectives may have a major impact on business activity and are designed to help the majority, not the minority.

 **Worked example**

Identify two features of an economic boom. (2)

One feature is increased customer demand; another is increased investment into businesses.

1 Low and stable price inflation

What is inflation? A sustained increase in the prices of the vast majority of goods and services available for sale in an economy. If inflation is increasing, it means the rate at which prices are rising is accelerating.

Why is high price inflation bad for business and an economy?

- As prices increase, consumers will not be able to afford to buy as many goods or services as they did before, so demand and sales will fall. This is because rising prices reduce **real incomes**. Real income is a measure of the purchasing power of money. If a person's income rises by 2 per cent but prices rise by 5 per cent, then that person's real income, and therefore the amount that he or she could have bought with it, will have fallen by 3 per cent.

- Business costs will increase as a result of the rising prices of the goods and services they purchase. Workers may also demand higher wages and salaries so they keep up with rising prices.

- The prices of goods produced in the economy will rise faster than those produced by firms located in countries with lower rates of inflation. As a result, consumers may buy cheaper products from firms located overseas instead. Businesses in the economy will lose sales and jobs will be lost.

Why control inflation? If a government can reduce price inflation and keep it low, it will make it easier for businesses to manage their costs, for exporters to sell their products overseas and for consumers, especially those on low incomes, to continue buying the goods and services they want and need.

2 High and stable employment

What is unemployment? People who are willing and able to work but are unable to find work because of a lack of suitable job opportunities.

Why is high unemployment bad for business and an economy?

- As unemployment rises, fewer people will be in work and so fewer goods and services will be produced. Total output in the economy will fall.

- Fewer people will be in paid work so total income will be lower. As a result, consumer spending will fall and businesses will lose revenue.

- The government may have to spend more on welfare or social security payments to support the unemployed and their families. Taxes on businesses and working people may be increased to pay for the additional government spending. This will reduce their disposable incomes and cause demand to fall.
  Alternatively, the government may have to cut spending on building roads, education or supporting new businesses.

- People who are unemployed for a long time may de-skill (lose their skills).

Why control employment? If a government can reduce unemployment and expand employment opportunities more people will be in paid work and earning regular incomes. As employment increases, total output will expand, consumer spending will rise, more business opportunities will be created and government spending on welfare can be reduced.

3 Economic growth in the national output and income

What is economic growth? An increase in the total output of goods and services in a national economy. The value of the total output of a national economy each year is measured by its **gross domestic product (GDP).**

Why is negative growth bad for business and an economy?

Many people are better off today than they were 20 or more years ago because most economies have experienced economic growth over time. However, steady economic growth may not be achieved every year. Sometimes economic growth can turn negative and when this happens the following will occur.

- There will be a sustained reduction in total output or GDP. Fewer people will be employed and so incomes and consumer spending will fall.
- Businesses will lose sales and profits. Many may be forced to close if consumer demand continues to fall.
- There will be fewer business opportunities. Entrepreneurs will not invest in new businesses and may move existing production to other countries where economic conditions are better.
- As incomes and profits fall, government revenue from taxes will fall and government spending on roads, schools and health care may have to be cut.

Why control economic growth? Sustained economic growth will create new business opportunities and jobs. Output, employment and incomes will rise and living standards will improve.

4 A favourable balance of international trade and payments

What is the balance of payments? International trade involves the exchange of goods, services and money between residents and firms located in different countries. The **balance of payments** of a country provides a record of the value of all its international trade and financial transactions with other countries.

Why is an unfavourable balance of international trade bad for business and an economy?

No country can produce everything its individual and business consumers need and want. Every country must therefore **import** some goods and services from other countries. In return, the sale of other goods and services to consumers overseas will earn foreign currency. This revenue from the sale of **exports** can therefore be used to pay for imported products.

If a country spends more on imports than it receives from the sale of exports, its balance of international payments will be in deficit. This can cause the following problems.

- The country may run out of foreign currency to buy imports and may have to borrow money from overseas.
- The national currency may lose value against other foreign currencies. This means it will be worth less than before and this will make imported goods and services more expensive to buy. In turn this can increase price inflation.
- Firms that need to import materials and parts from overseas to produce their own products will face rising costs.

Why control international trade and payments? A favourable balance of international trade and payments provides opportunities for businesses to expand their sales by exporting their goods and services to consumers overseas. It also provides jobs and incomes and ensures the economy can afford to import a wide variety of goods and services to satisfy consumer needs and wants.

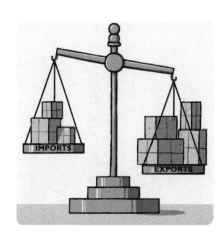

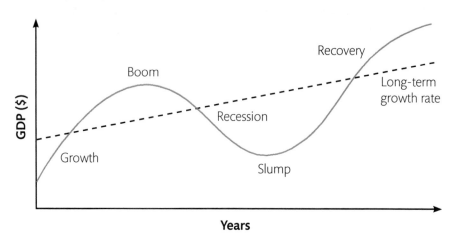

The business cycle

Figure 6.2 The business cycle

Stage of cycle	What happens?
GROWTH (expansion)	Business activity grows. Many businesses enjoy increased sales and profits. New businesses are formed. National output, incomes and employment increase.
BOOM (peak)	Consumer demand, sales and profits peak. There may be rapid inflation as prices rise quickly because consumer demand exceeds the amount of goods and services firms can produce and supply. The economy "overheats". Shortages of materials, parts and equipment increase business costs. Unemployment is low and wages rise as firms compete to employ skilled workers. The government may raise interest rates to control increasing inflation. Consumer confidence and spending may begin to decline due to high inflation and high interest rates.
RECESSION (downturn)	Consumer demand for many goods and services begins to fall. Business activity, sales and profits decline. There is a fall in total output (GDP) as sales decline and firms cut back production. Workers are made redundant and incomes fall, causing consumer spending to fall further. Many businesses cut back their demand for materials, parts and equipment. Total output falls further. Price inflation slows down. Prices may even begin to fall as businesses compete with each other to survive.
SLUMP (trough)	This is a deep and prolonged recession. Business activity, sales and profits may continue to fall or remain low. Many businesses are forced to close down. Unemployment is high and wages may be cut for those still in work. Many people experience falling living standards. The government may increase public spending, cut taxes and reduce interest rates to encourage consumer borrowing and spending.
RECOVERY (upturn)	Business and consumer confidence recovers. Spending on goods and services begins to rise. Sales and profits begin to rise. Firms increase output and employ more workers. New businesses are formed. Unemployment falls and incomes rise boosting consumer spending further. The economy starts to expand again.

Figure 6.3 A full business cycle goes through five main stages

The **business cycle** (see Figure 6.3) is a measure of the total annual value of all goods and services produced by business activity in a particular country.

The total value of an economy is called the **Gross Domestic Product (GDP)**.

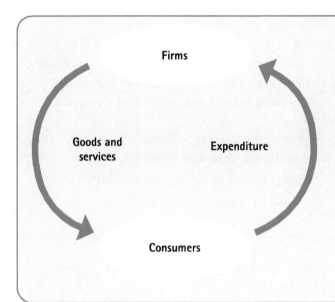

GDP measures the total value of all goods and services produced by business activity within a national economy each year. GDP is also, therefore, a measure of the national expenditure and national income of an economy.

This is because private and public sector organizations produce goods and services to sell to consumers. Revenue from the sale of goods and services is used by the owners of firms to pay wages and salaries to labour and to pay other firms and individuals to supply capital goods and natural resources. Any money left over after all these payments is profit. The total amount of wages, salaries, payments to suppliers of man-made and natural resources and profits in an economy make up its national income.

Businesses can be impacted by changes in the economic state of a country in many ways. Three main causes and their effects are shown below:

1. **Changing employment levels**
   - High levels of employment lead to increased consumer spending which increases demand and sales.
   - High employment means more demand and higher wages are needed, which reduces profits or increases costs.

2. **Changes in inflation**
   - Inflation means the costs of production rises, which increases prices and may reduce demand. This means employees need higher wages.
   - Unexpected or unplanned changes means businesses may make a loss if costs increase before prices are changed.

3. **Changes in GDP**
   - Rising GDP means more people are employed, confidence is high and finance is easy to find.
   - Falling GDP means confidence is falling, less people are spending money or investing and businesses cannot sell inventory.

 Apply

Create a life-cycle diagram for your country and see whether you can find reasons for changes in employment, inflation and GDP.

6.1.2 How control over the economy affects business activity and how business may respond

Economic policy instruments

In many countries, the government is usually a major investor, consumer and employer. This means governments use their influence to achieve economic objectives. The three main policy instruments governments use are explored in the table on the next page.

Factor	Reason
Public expenditure	• Finances from tax revenues and government borrowing. • Spent on major social and unprofitable projects. • May be awarded to private businesses via contracts for works or grants for research and investment. • Closely linked to taxes, as the more taxes that are generated, the more investment is affordable.
Taxes	• Taxes are used to collect finance for public expenditure, either directly from income and profit or indirectly from spending on goods and services. • Increasing tax reduces disposable income, so demand for luxury goods falls. • Reducing tax reduces the finance available for investment, so services are reduced. • Can be used to guide consumers towards healthy or environmental products and services and restrict access to imported or harmful products.
Interest rates	• Interest rates are the cost of borrowing money. • The main interest rate is set by the government or national bank, which influences what lending institutions can charge. • Raising interest rates increases the cost of borrowing, which reduces consumer spending and restricts demand for products and services, but reduces inflation. • Lowering interest rates decreases the cost of borrowing, encourages spending and investment and helps boost exports.

📖 Worked example

What is meant by 'public expenditure'? (2)

> Public expenditure is money spent by government authorities on providing necessary social amenities.

Direct and indirect taxes

Governments can use direct and indirect taxes to influence business activity and raise finances for public projects.

How much!!??!!

Tax category	Examples
Direct taxes – Taxes on goods and services, not income or profits	• VAT or sales tax is usually a percentage of the selling price. • Excise duty is a tax added at the point of production not sales. • Import tariffs are an additional amount charged on goods produced outside of the country.
Indirect taxes – Taxes on income and profits, not goods or services	• Personal income tax is usually a percentage of income. • Payroll taxes are additional taxes such as social security. • Corporation taxes are based on a company's profits.

Exam tip

Not all businesses suffer from raising tax levels: while luxury businesses may suffer, budget businesses often see a rise in demand and profits as shopping habits change.

The effects of changes in taxes

Figure 6.4 shows the effects changes in taxes can have on an economy.

Raising income tax
- Reduced disposable income
- Cutbacks on purchase of luxury goods and services
- Increased demand for essential and budget goods

Raising payroll tax
- Increases the cost of business and personal tax
- Increased cost of labour leads to more efficient working practices and redundancy
- Reduction in motivation and productivity of labour force

Raising corporation tax
- Less retained profit and reduced reward for investment
- Reduces enterprise and business investment
- Reduces expansion and research and development

Figure 6.4 *Changes to taxation policy can have far-reaching effects*

The effect of raising and lowering interest rates

Interest rates are often raised during **boom** periods. Interest rates are often lowered during periods of **recession**.

Effects of raising interest rates	Effects of lowering interest rates
Consumer spending may fall as the cost of borrowing rises	Consumer spending may increase as the cost of borrowing falls
Costs rise and investment falls	Costs fall and investment rises
The balance of international payments may become less favourable	The balance of international payments may become more favourable

Exam tip

Raising and lowering interest rates controls price inflation in a country and affects the affordability of goods and services.

 **Review**

Before you continue, make sure you are able to:

- understand how government control of the economy may affect business activity
- identify, explain and give examples of government objectives
- identify and explain the main stages of the business cycle
- explain how changes to tax and government spending may affect businesses
- identify and explain how interest rates affect business activity
- explain how businesses may respond to these changes.

You need to know about:
- environmental concerns and ethical issues
- the opportunities and constraints they present for businesses.

 Recap

As businesses produce goods and services, waste is also produced. This waste can cause damage to:

- the climate
- the health of the population
- wildlife.

Mass pollution of Earth's oceans reaches alarming levels

Global water supply drying up as population grows

China's vanishing land puts its crops and water supplies at risk

Pollution around cities Increases risk of cancer

Greenpeace says global beef trade destroying Amazon rainforest

Shark species face extinction amid over-fishing and appetite for fins

Visit the Maldives before they disappear

Research shows rising temperatures have already reduced rice yields in China, India, Thailand and other key farming locations by 10–20%.

Exam tip

Although sustainability is very expensive, it can be used in many ways by businesses, such as to reduce tax bills or for marketing purposes.

6.2.1 The relationship between business and the environment

Pollution can come from both production and consumption, for example:

- emissions such as carbon dioxide and other gases
- noise, air and water pollution
- chemical waste products.

 Worked example

Identify and explain two methods of sustainable development. (4)

One method would be to use using renewable energy, as it reduces the use of valuable or scarce energy resources. Another would be to recycle, to make more efficient use of resources.

As the world grows, more people manufacture and consume products. This increases the scale of the problems and solutions need to be found.

Sustainable development

Sustainable development is an important issue in today's business environment.

Sustainable development is about finding ways to grow businesses while reducing or eliminating the effect of this growth on the environment. This may include:

- using **renewable energy** instead of fossil fuels
- increasing **recycling** and reuse to make more efficient use of resources
- reducing waste such as packaging to reduce plastic pollution
- increased use of biodegradable materials which do not damage the environment
- remanufacturing and reusing items to extend the lifespan of damaging materials.

Positive and negative externalities

Most businesses are focused on creating wealth for their shareholders and may be unaware or uninterested in the effects their activities have on other stakeholders.

However, if a business focuses on more than one stakeholder, they may have positive or beneficial impacts on others – **positive externalities**. An example of this is shown in Figure 6.5.

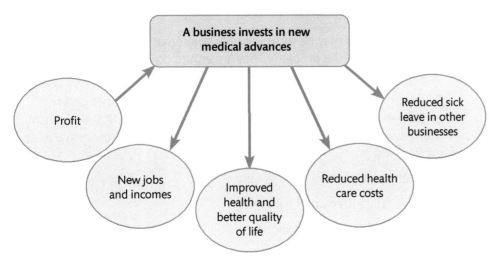

Figure 6.5 *How some business activities can create wider social and economic benefits*

Businesses may often cause **negative externalities** on others. These are likely to be social, environmental or economic.

Negative externalities may add to external costs, not just to a business owner but also to other stakeholders. These costs may include:

- loss of revenue
- compensation costs
- loss of wildlife or long-term damage to the environment
- pollution.

Environmental pressures and opportunities

There are many different factors that can influence or put pressure on business activities (Figure 6.6).

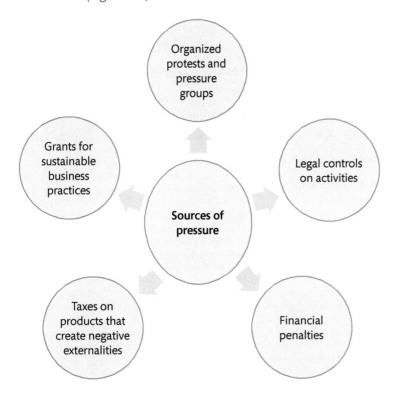

Figure 6.6 *Pressure to improve environmental policies can have radical effects on the way businesses operate*

> **Apply**
>
> Create a matching exercise with businesses in section A and externalities in section B. Challenge your friends to match the correct externalities to the business.

> **Exam tip**
>
> Acting ethically may be a net gain to a business if the business can market their activities successfully and build customer loyalty.

Pressure groups

Pressure groups may be local, national or international depending on the size and scope of the problem. They are groups organized to counter the negative impacts of business on the environment or society.

Pressure groups often aim to create negative publicity and persuade consumers to boycott certain products. However, they may also highlight businesses that have taken or are taking action to reduce their negative externalities.

To be effective, pressure groups must:

- be well organized and financed
- have significant public support
- receive regular TV and press coverage
- be able to prove businesses are acting illegally or unethically.

Legal and other government controls

Governments may introduce laws and regulations forcing businesses to reduce negative externalities. Common legal controls are:

- anti-pollution laws
- planning and building regulations
- regulation of the use and phasing out of harmful products
- emissions standards and controls.

Taxes may also be introduced to increase the prices of harmful products. This leads to:

- a reduction in the number of sales
- a reduction in the profitability of goods
- an increase in recycling and 'greener' products
- reorganization of business objectives and outputs.

Grants may be introduced to lower the cost of sustainable products. This leads to:

- increased research and development into new technologies and products
- renewable products and services
- positive externalities.

6.2.2 Ethical issues

Ethical issues are now becoming more important among stakeholders due to increased publicity. However, acting ethically increases business costs, which may cause conflict with shareholders.

Child labour is a very important ethical issue for manufacturing businesses. There are two options a business must consider: to continue using suppliers which may use child labour, or to find suppliers who do not use child labour.

Ethical behaviour can bring significant benefits to a business. It can help to:

- attract more customers to the business, boosting sales and profits
- attract and retain the most talented and productive employees, thereby reducing labour turnover and recruitment costs
- attract new investors, providing low-cost capital to finance business expansion.

 Recap

Ethics is the judgment of what is right or wrong. They include the values, standards and morals that govern how society behaves.

 **Review**

Before you continue, make sure you are able to:

- understand how environmental concerns and ethical issues can create both opportunities and constraints for business
- show how business activity can impact on the environment
- understand the concept of the externalities of a business
- describe how business activity can contribute to sustainable development
- explain how businesses may respond to environmental pressures, opportunities and pressure groups
- explain how legal controls affect business and the business environment
- explain the ethical issues of businesses and how businesses may respond to ethical issues.

You need to know:
- the importance of globalization
- reasons for the importance and growth of multinational companies
- the impact of exchange rates.

 Recap

Globalization is the expansion of the global economy, which leads to increased trade and business opportunities. Globalization refers to easier interconnections and interactions between people, businesses and governments worldwide.

Exam tip

Many people refer to the world 'getting smaller' as communications and travel is much easier and cheaper than it used to be.

6.3.1 The importance of globalization

The concept of globalization

Globalization is increasing due to:

- an increased global population, which leads to more potential customers
- rising output, employment and incomes increasing consumer spending
- improvements in the speed and cost of international communications
- easier migration for work purposes – especially for multinational businesses.

International trade involves exchanging goods, services and money across national borders:

- exports are goods and services sold to consumers in other countries
- imports are goods and services of one country that are purchased by consumers from another.

Some of the opportunities and threats associated with globalization are shown below.

Opportunities for businesses in an economy created by globalization and international trade	Potential threats to businesses in an economy from globalization and international trade
✓ The ability to import goods and services from overseas allows businesses in an economy to specialize in products they are best able to produce and to export them all over the world.	✗ Increased competition from cheaper imports may reduce the sales and profits of new and established businesses making the same or similar products. Those unable to increase their efficiency and lower their costs may eventually be forced out of business.
✓ Businesses may increase their revenues and profits through the sale of exports to consumers overseas. Businesses able to do so will be able to expand their production and benefit from economies of scale.	✗ There will be increased competition for sales and skilled employees from overseas organizations that have located business operations in the economy.
✓ Businesses may also find it easier to expand by opening additional business premises overseas to make and sell their products near to new consumer markets. Some may relocate all their production overseas to countries where wages, other costs and taxes are lower.	✗ New and established businesses may find it increasingly difficult to attract and retain highly skilled employees if new and better paid opportunities to work overseas are created. Wages may have to rise to retain skilled workers.
✓ New business opportunities will be created in the distribution and retailing industries from the importation and sale of items produced overseas.	✗ It may become more difficult for new and established businesses to raise capital if investors are attracted to new and more profitable business opportunities overseas.
✓ Business organizations that find it difficult to fill their job vacancies may be able to advertise and recruit skilled labour from overseas.	✗ Business closures due to competition with cheap imports, business relocation overseas and a loss of capital to support new start-ups will result in a loss of output, jobs and incomes in the economy.
✓ Businesses may be able to import the latest technologies, and the materials and components they need for more efficient production, from cheaper suppliers overseas.	

Trade barriers

Governments may try to protect national output and employment opportunities from overseas competition.

Governments may try to restrict international competition for three main reasons:

- to protect small businesses, new and emerging industries and employment opportunities
- to prevent the dumping of stock that is obsolete or illegal in the home country
- to improve the balance of international trade and payments.

Governments may use some or all of the **protectionist** policy instruments below:

- **Import tariffs** – indirect taxes on imported goods to make domestic goods cheaper
- **Quotas** – limits on the quantities of products imported to increase demand and selling price
- **Subsidies** – payments to local firms to reduce production costs and selling prices
- **Embargoes** – total bans on certain or all goods from a particular country.

 Worked example

Identify two possible outcomes of using trade barriers. (2)

Costs may rise for importers; a reduction in the dumping of obsolete goods.

Drawbacks of trade barriers

While there may be benefits of **trade barriers**, there may also be drawbacks. These include:

- rising costs and/or supply shortages for businesses dependent on imported materials
- the growth of inefficient businesses that produce low-quality or high-cost goods
- a lack of choice and higher prices for domestic customers
- reciprocal trade barriers from other countries, which may harm exports.

Exam tip

Trade barriers are often used by developing countries to make sure that small domestic companies are not destroyed, as the country will then have to rely on multinational companies for jobs and the economy.

6.3.2 Reasons for the importance and growth of multinational companies

The benefits of being an MNC

 Recap

Multinational companies (MNCs) operate in more than one country and are some of the largest companies in the world. MNCs often have headquarters in one country and subsidiary companies that produce goods and services in other countries. They often employ thousands of people globally and revenues may even be greater than the total income of many countries.

Key advantages of being an MNC are shown in Figure 6.7.

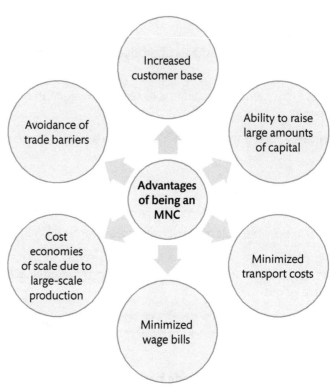

Figure 6.7 *Multinational corporations enjoy a variety of benefits not available to smaller businesses*

Exam tip

A business may want to expand via **foreign direct investment (FDI)** as this allows complete control of the business as well as gaining significant trade and economic advantages.

Exam tip

MNCs can also be referred to as global businesses and benefit from economies of scale due to their size.

The impact of MNCs on stakeholders

There are many impacts, both positive and negative, on various stakeholders.

Advantages	Disadvantages
✓ Less competition	✘ Limited opportunities for sales and growth
✓ Lower costs as product quality is more important than advertising	
	✘ Often relies on one customer segment, so a change in consumer buying habits may cause business failure
✓ Attracts high-value customers	
✓ Creates a reputation of specialism	

Positive impacts	Negative impacts
Provision of jobs, income and reduced unemployment	May force local competitors out of business
Capital investment into premises and equipment, which boosts economic growth	Movement of profits reduces tax bills within countries
Increased variety of goods and services forces domestic producers to improve efficiency	MNCs may demand subsidies and tax advantages to invest
New ideas, technology and skills	Exploitation of workers in low-wage economies
Taxes paid on profits increase national revenue and available finance	MNCs may exploit natural resources and damage the environment

 Worked example

Identify and explain two disadvantages of an MNC opening a subsidiary in a new country. (6)

> One disadvantage would be reduced sales for similar local businesses. The MNC will have greater cost efficiencies of scales, which means they will have lower costs per unit. Another disadvantage would be the repatriation of profits. As the MNC's headquarters are in another country, any profits leave the host country, and there is less investment.

6.3.3 The impact of exchange rates

Foreign exchange markets

 Recap

International trade requires financial transactions in different national currencies. A business must therefore be aware of the exchange rate when buying or selling goods and services overseas, and the potential effect on costs, revenue and profits.

International trade affects any businesses that take part in the activities shown below.

Imports	• imports materials, components or finished goods from organizations overseas • buys services from overseas suppliers
Exports	• exports materials, components or finished goods to business, government or individual consumers overseas • sells services to business, government or individual consumers overseas
Investments	• buys shares in the ownership of overseas companies • invests in premises and equipment to start and run business units in other countries

Exam tip

A business that exports has the choice to sell in either the domestic currency or the foreign currency – each has its own risks and advantages.

Depreciation and appreciation of an exchange rate

Governments may try to control or fix the exchange rate of the national currency to give themselves a financial advantage, but most have floating exchange rates, which means they vary depending on global demand for the currency. These variances are called **appreciation** and **depreciation**.

A currency might depreciate because...	A currency might appreciate because...
• the country buys more imports than it exports. To do so it must sell its currency to buy other currencies.	• the country sells more exports than it imports. Overseas consumers must sell their currencies to buy exports from that country.
• interest rates fall relative to those in other countries so people move their savings to banks overseas.	• interest rates rise relative to those in other countries. This attracts savings from overseas residents.
• inflation rises relative to inflation in other countries. This makes exports more expensive. Overseas demand for them, and the currency needed to buy them, will fall.	• inflation is lower than in other countries so exports will become more competitive. Overseas demand for them, and the currency required to pay for them, will rise.
• people and businesses speculate their national currency will fall in value and sell their holdings of the currency.	• people and businesses speculate their national currency will rise in value and buy more of the currency.

 Worked example

Do you think an importing business should be worried about an appreciation in the exchange rate of their currency? Justify your answer. (6)

No, I do not think they should be worried, as the rise in the value of their currency will reduce the cost of imports relative to the price of other items produced by domestic companies, which will improve their competitiveness and reduce prices, increasing sales revenue and profitability.

 Apply

Write and film a news report which describes the effect of MNCs on the national economy.

The effect of appreciating exchange rates on businesses

Small changes in **exchange rates** will affect the competitiveness of exports from one country to another. International competitiveness impacts on costs, revenues and profits depending on whether or not a business imports or exports goods internationally.

Appreciation of domestic currency in the foreign exchange market ⇒ The selling price of exported products has to rise to cover costs ⇒ International competitiveness reduced and international demand could fall ⇒ This reduces the revenue and profits of the exporting company

Figure 6.8 *The effect of changes in domestic currency on a business's exports to international markets*

Appreciation of domestic currency in the foreign exchange market ⇒ The purchase price of international goods reduces ⇒ The competitiveness of imports increases and demand for imports increases ⇒ This reduces the costs of materials and improves the competitiveness of the importer as selling prices reduce

Figure 6.9 *The effect of changes in domestic currency on a business's imports from international markets*

The effect of depreciating exchange rates on businesses

As exchange rates depreciate, the opposite happens for domestic businesses. Figure 6.10 shows an example of this from Iran and Germany.

> The Hassas Export Co., based in Tehran, is one of Iran's leading exporters of pistachio nuts and each month sends around 4000 tonnes to Germany. Its exports compete internationally with pistachio nuts exported from the US and Turkey.

> Atrimex Gmbh in Hamburg Germany is a major importer of pistachios to sell to food processing companies and retail outlets all over Europe. To pay for the nuts it imports from the Hassas Export Co., it needs to exchange the European currency, the euro (€), for Iranian rials.

Iran sells pistachio nuts to Germany

Germany pays for nuts with Iranian rials

Iran sells Iranian rials on foreign exchange market

Germany buys rials with euros

IRAN   **GERMANY**

Figure 6.10 *Increased foreign demand causes costs to export customers to fall and the exchange rate to depreciate*

Exam tip

It is important to understand that with exchange rates, when importers benefit, exporters lose, and vice versa.

Review

Before you continue, make sure you are able to:

- understand the concept of and reasons for globalization
- explain the opportunities and threats of globalization for business
- explain why some governments introduce import tariffs and quotas
- identify the importance of and reasons for the growth of MNCs
- explain the benefits of becoming a multinational business
- list the potential benefits and drawbacks of MNCs to a country or economy
- understand the impact of changes in exchange rates on businesses
- explain depreciation and appreciation of an exchange rate
- explain how exchange rates can affect different types of businesses.

Exam-style questions

Unit 6

An MNC manufactures furniture in 10 countries across the world and is headquartered in a country which has a high cost of living.

The finance director is worried about the effect of changing exchange rates, the impact of external influences, such as increasing environmental awareness, and the impact of these issues on profits.

The MNC purchases its raw materials globally and exports products to 25 countries worldwide.

(a) Identify two negative externalities of business activity on the environment. (2)

(b) Identify two reasons why the finance director might be worried about changing exchange rates. (2)

(c) Explain the term 'exchange rates'. (2)

(d) Explain the term 'external influences'. (2)

(e) Identify and explain two possible reasons why the MNC might have chosen to manufacture in 10 countries. (4)

(f) Identify and explain two reasons why the MNC purchases raw materials globally. (4)

(g) Identify and explain two reasons why increasing environmental awareness may impact the MNC's profits. (4)

(h) Identify and explain two factors the MNC should consider when responding to environmental pressures. (6)

(i) Do you think that fluctuating exchange rates will affect the MNC? Justify your answer. (6)

Exam tip

In questions like (i), remember that the answer 'yes' or 'no' doesn't matter as much as how you explain and justify your decision.

7.1 How to achieve the best possible result in your Business Studies examinations

Study time is important. However, it is even more important to make good use of your study time.

Recent research shows that there are some important things you can do from the very start to make sure you achieve your best.

The first thing is to set yourself some definite goals. Here are some important questions which may help you to plan your approach to study:

Question 1

What grade do you want (or need) to achieve in your Business Studies exam? What grade will be worth all the effort over the last two years, and will allow you to progress to the next stage in your education or employment?

Setting yourself a specific target may motivate you to study not only your revision notes but also the grade descriptors.

Question 2

How much extracurricular time do you spend developing your knowledge and skills in business?

Maybe you already spend many hours a week in private study, but if this is not the case, it is a good idea to increase your study time.

This can be done gradually – for example, you could plan to add an extra hour to your normal study time for the next two weeks, then add an extra hour to this increased time, and so on.

Question 3

What is your reaction when a piece of work from your Business Studies course is returned by the teacher and you have not done quite as well as you had hoped, despite having made a real effort?

You may feel a bit deflated if you just focus on the negative comments. However, you could think a little differently by focusing on the learning points. Students who reflect on their performance are able to turn a negative experience into something far more positive, which then leads to real progress.

Question 4

What do you do with all the work completed during your course of study?

Students usually find it helpful to keep a carefully organized collection of the work they do.

Have a separate section for each topic with your notes and all the answers you have prepared, together with the questions.

When preparing for the examination, having a well-organized file will mean you can get on with revision without wasting time trying to find the relevant materials.

 **Review**

At this stage, you should:

- have a definite goal (the final grade you would like to achieve)

- have a plan to increase the time spent on private study

- view each result you achieve as an opportunity to learn from your mistakes

- be building up a file of work which will be invaluable for revision.

7.2 Practical ideas to help you learn more effectively

Self-assessment

Self-assessment means that you mark your own work using model answers or mark schemes provided with past examination papers.

Research has shown that there are many benefits of self-assessment if you carry out the process regularly. For example, you will:

- find out for yourself how well you have done after completing a task

- get immediate information about errors or omissions in your answer

- learn exactly how marks are allocated to answers, so that you are better prepared to produce the answers expected in exam situations.

Peer assessment

By marking a friend's practice exam answer, **peer assessing** can not only help identify errors and omissions your friends have made, but can also challenge you to write down obvious answers or explanations.

'Repairing' your answers

The more substantial benefits of checking your own work appear when you then go on to analyse missing or incorrect information in your answer.

It is a good idea to try to understand why the model answer is showing an outcome that is different to the answer you have provided.

Try and work out for yourself how the right answer was achieved, or maybe ask your teacher or a friend to explain the right answer to you.

Add some notes about the correct answer to your work; these will be useful when you look back at the question, and may also help you to remember the points in your exam.

Below you will find some examples illustrating how to **repair** answers.

 Worked example

Repairing an answer where a calculation is incorrect

Calculate the current ratio in 2018 using the information provided in the table. (2)

Product x	Amount ($)
Raw materials	100
Current assets	750
Current liabilities	250

Student answer	Model answer
To work out the current ratio you must take away the raw materials from the current assets and then divide the answer by the current liabilities. This is: $(750 - 100)/250 = 2.6 : 1$	$\dfrac{\textit{Current assets} - \textit{raw materials}}{\textit{Current liabilities}} \times 100$ $\dfrac{750 - 100}{250} \times 100 = 2.6 : 1$

Repaired answer

To work out the current ratio you must ~~take away the raw materials from~~ divide the current assets ~~and then divide the answer~~ by the current liabilities.

The original answer calculated the acid-test ratio.

$$\frac{Current\ assets - raw\ materials}{Current\ liabilities} \times 100$$

$$\frac{750 - 100}{250} \times 100 = 3:1$$

You should always check your answer to make sure the figure is correct.

 Worked example

Repairing an answer with an incorrectly written response
Identify and explain two methods of selection for the position of shop manager. (8)

Student answer	Model answer
One appropriate method could be a work trial, where the manager is given a basic task to complete. Another is an interview where questions are asked about the role the manager will complete.	An appropriate method of selection is a work trail. This allows the recruiter to see if the recruit is able to complete the manager's daily tasks. However, a recruit may be nervous and not complete the tasks to the best of their ability.

Student answer	Repair
One appropriate method could be a work trial, where the manager is given a basic task to complete. Another is an interview where questions are asked about the role the manager will complete.	Instead of listing many of the methods of selection I know, I should have focused on some I know well, and given analysis for each one. This then shows my ability to analyse, which allows me to reach the top grades in an 8-mark answer.

Why is assessing my own work and then 'repairing' answers such a good idea?

Research has shown that this 'repairing' approach will make a big difference to what a student can gain from all the practical work. Over a course of study, it can boost an individual's performance by as much as two examination grades.

In the first example, the student has chosen the incorrect calculation when creating the ratio answer. If this process is repeated whenever this type of error is made, then it is likely the student will learn the correct formula.

In the second example, the student has focused attention on delivering knowledge instead of providing analysis, which is the important part of the question. The student now has a personal record of what is needed to avoid repeating the error.

If the student repeats this process for similar questions, it is likely they will remember this distinction between a knowledge question and an analysis question.

Remember: each correction you make represents a step towards improving your examination performance.

7.3 Making progress with written answers

To boost your ability to demonstrate knowledge, understanding and analysis of key ideas and concepts, you could try the following process when you are reading through a passage in a textbook, a handout or case study about a particular topic.

The process helps you organize information and consists of several steps:

1. Highlight key points in the text.

2. Prepare a table in which you make notes which summarize key points about a particular aspect of the topic.

3. Prepare a second table, this time making notes which summarize key points about a different aspect of the topic, and so on. More tables can be added if necessary.

Using tables to analyse knowledge and ideas

Having highlighted key points in a textbook about the key methods of motivation, you could produce tables like the ones below, which look at methods of motivation for work.

Method	Definition	Application
Financial reward e.g. wage, salary bonus, commission, profit share	A method of motivation which gives monetary rewards for achieving set targets.	Used for factory settings where the management uses Taylor's scientific management theory.
Non-financial reward e.g. job enrichment and rotation, teamworking, training, promotion	A method of motivation which brings emotional and psychological rewards for achievement.	Useful for skilled and experienced employees who use Maslow's and Herzberg's theories of motivation.

Method	Advantage	Disadvantage
Financial reward	Employees receive a direct monetary reward for the work they have produced.	May limit motivation if targets are set too high or are unachievable.
Non-financial reward	Employees have a sense of well-being and involvement with the business, which increases loyalty and happiness.	Some employees may feel undervalued if there are no financial rewards and may not be motivated.

The next table may look at specific situations in which the methods of motivation would be most or least effective, with reasons.

This process of building layers of knowledge and analysis in tables with a clear focus can be a powerful study tool. It makes information easily accessible and it can be separated into subject-specific elements.

7.4 Avoiding the most common exam errors

From reading the exam tips in this exam study guide, you will be well aware of a number of key errors made by students. It is important that you know how to avoid some of the most common errors in examination answers.

✗ Common error 1: misreading questions

Although you may have read the question once, have you understood what it is asking you to do, and how many marks are allocated? It may be useful to highlight key pieces of text before you start your answer to make sure that you have fully understood the question.

When the question asks about 'recruitment':

- is it asking for methods of recruitment or recruitment strategies, for example?
- is it asking you to analyse one method or strategy, or is it only asking to analyse the advantages?

Make sure you answer the question that was asked.

✗ Common error 2: not looking at the number of marks allocated

Students who run out of time often have not looked at the amount of marks allocated to a question. This is obvious when a 3-mark 'briefly explain' question may have an answer which is written over one or two whole pages.

This not only wastes valuable time in an exam, but may also make it harder for an examiner to correctly allocate the marks, as the key points can be hidden in a long essay-type answer.

Then, for the last questions, the student is forced to use bullet points, which means it is very difficult to gain analysis marks.

Make sure you understand what is required from each question.

✗ Common error 3: not identifying the 'command' word

This is closely linked to common error 2. Candidates often focus on the content element in the question – such as business objectives or the size of the business. While this important, it is also vital to look carefully at the command word being used, as this indicates what the examiner is actually asking you to do.

For example:

- 'State' or 'define' only requires basic knowledge which can easily be answered in a few short sentences.
- 'Analyse' will require the candidate to look at the advantages or disadvantages, strengths or weaknesses.
- 'Discuss' requires the candidate to make a judgment based on the preceding analysis. The student must usually make a decision about what is the 'most suitable'. This must be based on a two-sided analysis. A strong answer will compare the strongest with the second and third options.

Make sure you identify the command word.

✗ Common error 4: incorrect or poor answer structure

Although it is understandable that students may rush answers within an exam setting, it is important to remember that there is always enough time to answer all the questions set.

However, it is also important to realize that the exam is not the best place to start learning how to structure an answer. It may be useful to use revision tables, which are linked to the type of question set.

7.5 Example questions and mark schemes

Two-mark questions

 Worked example

Define the term 'sole trader'. (2)

> A business owned by one person who has unlimited liability.

Two-mark questions will use 'command' words such as 'define', 'state' or 'identify' and will need basic knowledge with one form of expanded answer.

	Answer	Marker's explanation
Mark 1	A business owned by one person	This is a simple definition, but the most important aspect
Mark 2	who has unlimited liability	This expands the point

Four-mark questions

 Worked example

Identify and explain two methods of recruitment. (4)

> Using recruitment agencies who specialize in helping businesses recruit the staff they need.
>
> Headhunting from other organizations, which means identifying and approaching the person you want who works in another organization.

Whereas four-mark questions, usually found on Paper 1 (the first paper you sit) will usually begin with 'Identify and explain two...' and will usually need **one piece** of explanation in context for each point.

	Answer	Marker's explanation
Mark 1	Using recruitment agencies	This is a simple definition, but the most important aspect
Mark 2	who specialize in helping businesses recruit the staff they need.	This expands the point with a simple point.
Mark 3	Headhunting from other organizations	This is a simple definition, but the most important aspect
Mark 4	which is identifying and approaching the person you want who works in another organization.	This expands the point with a simple point.

Six-mark questions

 Worked example

Identify, explain and analyse two methods of recruitment an MNC should use. (6)

> The MNC should use recruitment agencies because it can fill its urgent positions quickly, as recruitment agencies have records of people available to work immediately. The MNC could also headhunt candidates from other organizations as the MNC needs an experienced manager and it can find the person that is required with the experience needed.

Six-mark questions, will usually begin with 'Identify, explain and analyse two…' and will usually need one piece of analysis in context for each point.

	Answer	Marker's explanation
Mark 1	The MNC should use recruitment agencies	This is a simple definition, but the most important aspect
Mark 2	because it can fill its urgent positions quickly,	This is a relevant reference to the short case study
Mark 3	as recruitment agencies have records of people available to work immediately.	This is the analytical point required
Mark 4	The MNC could also headhunt candidates from other organizations	This is a simple definition, but the most important aspect
Mark 5	as the MNC needs an experienced manager	This is a relevant reference to the short case study
Mark 6	and it can find the person that is required with the experience needed.	This is the analytical point required

In other cases, you will be given a statement, with the question 'Do you agree? Justify your answer'. This will usually need one piece of knowledge and application, with 2 marks each for analysis and evaluation. The evidence (e.g. the MNC) is an example of using a case study to support an answer.

	Answer	Marker's explanation
Mark 1	A headhunter will be able to find a candidate with the right skills and experience	This is a simple definition, but the most important aspect
Mark 2	which is important, as the MNC's employees are unhappy and unmotivated.	This is a relevant reference to the short case study
Mark 3	An experienced headhunter will be able to solve the MNC's problems and increase motivation	This is a positive analytical point
Mark 4	but the experienced manager will want a higher salary than in his/her last job, which will be expensive.	This is a negative analytical point
Mark 5	The MNC should use a headhunter, as this will solve the problem quickly	A judgment is made…
Mark 6	and increase productivity and be worth the high salary.	…and further developed

Eight-mark questions

 Worked example

Identify and explain two sources of finance for an MNC's new premises. (8)

> A mortgage is used for buildings as a large amount can be paid off over many years, which is suitable for the MNC, as the cost of the new building is very large, and their predicted revenue will cover the mortgage cost. Increasing share capital is suitable as the investment will not have to be repaid, which is suitable as the MNC wished to invest future profits into research and development and will save on the cost of the interest, which is 5 per cent.

Eight-mark questions are found on Paper 2, and may begin with 'Identify and explain two ways...'

Although the question is the same as a 4-mark question on Paper 1, the marks awarded are higher, which means that more information is required.

	Answer	Marker's explanation
Knowledge Mark 1	A mortgage	This is a simple answer which is suitable for the option
Analysis Mark 2	is used for buildings as a large amount can be paid off over many years,	This is a piece of basic analysis
Application Marks 3 and 4	which is suitable for the MNC, as the cost of the new building is very large, and their predicted revenue will cover the mortgage cost.	Two application marks are awarded for each benefit
Knowledge Mark 5	Increasing share capital	This is a simple answer which is suitable for the option
Analysis Mark 6	is suitable as the investment will not have to be repaid,	This is a piece of basic analysis
Application Marks 7 and 8	which is suitable as the MNC wished to invest future profits into research and development and will save on the cost of the interest, which is 5 per cent.	Two application marks are awarded for each benefit

It is important to select the most appropriate sources in this question. An overdraft would not be considered suitable, as it is a short-term method used for emergencies only.

An MNC has created a new model of car. They must consider the price, place and promotion. Which will be the most important factor when deciding a final strategy? Justify your answer. (8)

On Paper 2, each question B is usually marked out of 12. However, these questions have a slightly different marking scale, as it is marked on achievement of three levels.

	Criteria	Marker's explanation
Level 3 **7-10 marks**	There must be at least two marks awarded at the Level 2 stage to access Level 3. A justified conclusion as to the most important factor and why the other options were not chosen. Limited judgment as to the most important factor.	This requires evaluation of the analysis at Level 2
Level 2 **4-6 marks**	Discussion of each factor affecting the final strategy (1 per factor).	This requires each factor at Level 1 to be analysed in context
Level 1 **0-3 marks**	Three factors outlined with evidence from the text (one per factor).	This requires three factors in context to be identified

It is important to understand the importance and use of connecting phrases, such as:

- 'which means'
- 'this leads to'.

Using these is what will allow the student to reach Level 2.

An additional 2 marks awarded for relevant application.

 Review

Make sure you remember to:

- read the questions carefully and correctly
- make a note of the number of marks awarded
- identify the 'command' word
- structure your answer appropriately to the question and the exam paper.

7.6 Understanding what is expected by different types of question

Each question in an exam will start with a particular 'command' word which asks you to do something. It is important to understand why particular words are used and what they mean, otherwise it is possible you will waste time by misunderstanding what is required and lose marks by not doing what is expected of you.

'Command' word	What is being tested
Identify, state, define	Knowledge
Describe, briefly explain	Understanding
Explain, calculate	Application of knowledge or the case study material
Analyse	Ability to analyse elements of the course
Discuss, justify, assess, evaluate, recommend	Ability to look at a situation or a problem from different points of view, consider a range of factors, make a judgment and provide a conclusion

'Command' word	What is expected	Examples of questions
Identify, state, define	A brief response that shows you can remember basic facts and ideas.	**Identify** two management styles. **State** two business objectives. **Define** marketing.
Explain, calculate	Answers are required about a particular situation, using extended knowledge or data.	**Explain** the difference between a fixed and variable cost. **Calculate** the acid-test ratio.
Identify and explain	Study information in depth, separating out different aspects of the information and analysing key benefits and drawbacks.	**Identify and explain** two benefits of reducing inventory.
Discuss, justify	Make a judgment and give reasons to support a particular proposal or idea, highlighting key benefits and drawbacks.	**Discuss** the most appropriate methods of selection. **Justify** the most appropriate marketing strategy for an MNC.

7.7 Exam preparation

Exam preparation begins long before the day of the exam. Organization is key, and below are some tops tips to success:

1. Make sure your notes are well organized and you can easily find them.

2. Make sure you have practiced past papers. Don't look at the final mark, but at what you didn't do so well on, and how you lost marks.

3. When doing exam practice scripts, always time yourself! There is no point in doing a practice exam in two hours when the real one only lasts for 90 minutes.

4. Make sure you have one good, up-to-date course book which will give you hints, tips and the basic knowledge needed to succeed in your business exam.

5. Keep up to date with news and new developments. This is especially important for Paper 1, where you need to show application to relevant examples.

6. Download a copy of the syllabus and make a checklist; use a highlighter to check off what you are confident in and where you have a lack of knowledge.

7. Get a study buddy. It is much easier to study when you know there is somebody else with you.

8. Revise sensibly and practice all your skills. If you focus only on knowledge, you may end up losing marks in the long-answer questions.

9. Create model answers and structures you can use in your exams. Remember, examiners are not trying to trick you, so if you can focus on the subject, that will help you to relax and give good answers.

10. Understand what the examiner will be looking for and try to focus your attention on meeting those requirements. The key concepts below will help.

Key concepts

Studying business should not just mean being able to remember lots of facts and being able to analyse effectively. It should help you to make links between topics and develop a deep and meaningful relationship with the topic.

These key concepts of business are designed to help focus your mind on the most important elements.

Key concepts	Description
Change	Often described as the only constant, students of business must realize that business can only develop and grow with change. Change is good!
Management	Good leadership should mean a highly motivated workforce, effective systems and an efficient method of communication.
Customer focus	Without customers, businesses would not exist, therefore, customers should be understood and their needs and wants met.
Innovation	Reinvention is the only way that a business can stay ahead of its competitors. As times change, so must the business.
Creating value	Businesses exist to meet the needs of their stakeholders. These could be either the shareholders or the recipients of social enterprise. Businesses must create and measure value.
Strategy	If you know where you are and where you want to get to, you should then be able to create a plan to achieve your long-term goals.

7.8 The exam

You have studied, you know the key concepts, your notes are excellent... now it's the exam!

Rule number 1: don't panic!

You've spent a full year studying, revising and living the subject – you know what you need to do and there are no tricks. Show the examiners how good you are.

Rule number 2: read the instructions and the questions carefully

Don't overlook any details, don't rush to be the first one to finish and make sure you have time to review your answers.

Rule number 3: manage your time

You know how much time you have, you know how long each question should take and there is a clock in the exam hall. Do not run out of time and do not rush questions.

Rule number 4: remember this is a business exam

You have spent the last year learning business terminology, rules and methods. Use this vocabulary to show your deeper understanding of the subject.

Rule number 5: follow the order of the questions

Students who mix up the order of the questions often miss out entire questions. This therefore means they cannot score maximum marks. Questions are also laid out to make sense, and information in one question may help in the following questions.

Time management

Paper 1

You have 1 hour and 30 minutes to complete four sections. Each section is based on a mini case study and is separated into questions A to E.

Questions A and B consist of generic, short-answer questions which do not require the use of the case study.

Questions C and D consists of one short-answer question, often asking for two examples or reasons for factors in relation to the case study. Each point must be explained **in the context of the short case study.** A generic explanation may only score 2 out of the 4 marks available.

Question E consists of one long-answer question, often asking for your opinion on whether a business should choose or reject an option or pathway. All answers must be **in the context of the short case study.** A generic explanation may only score two out of the six marks available.

Paper 2

You have 1 hour and 30 minutes to complete four questions, each worth 20 marks. Each question is separated into parts A and B (sometimes there may also be a part C). An insert with a case study must be used as evidence for all four questions.

It is recommended that you do not spend more than 20 minutes on each question. However, this is only a guide. You may need to spend more time on one question and less on another. As long as you are aware of the time available and the questions left, then you should be able to allocate your time appropriately.

7.9 Skills unit

There are some generic-level descriptors that are used – basic understanding, outline or knowledge, discussion or analysis, and judgment/ developed recommendation.

It can often be difficult to determine whether a candidate answer is outlined or discussed. A good way is to imagine a tennis ball – if you throw a tennis ball and it hits the ground and stops, this is disappointing; you want the ball to bounce and go further.

- This first element is usually basic understanding or knowledge:
    - o this is often a simple, learnt definition.

- The only way to make the ball go further is to pick up the ball and throw it again:
    - o a candidate does this in an exam by writing multiple, unconnected statements, such as a list or simple bullet points.

If you throw the ball, it hits the ground and bounces. This is better, as the ball goes further. However, the ball does not bounce again.

- This is now considered to be discussion:
    - o this is when a candidate explains their learnt statement or applies the theory to an example
    - o a candidate does this by using a connecting word, such as 'because', 'which means' or 'an effect of this is'.

If the ball bounces more than once, it goes further. The more it bounces, the happier the candidate and the examiner will be.

- This is now considered to be discussion:
    - o this occurs when a candidate shows a depth of understanding which is more than mere knowledge or simple consequences
    - o a candidate does this by using more than one connecting word, e.g. 'because of X, Y happens, which can lead to Z' or 'if X occurs, then Y is the result, which affects the business in Z'.

If the ball is compared to a different type of ball and a decision is made to the best or most suitable type of ball, the happier the candidate and the examiner will be.

- This is now considered to be judgment:
    - o this occurs when a candidate shows an ability to make a decision on the best or most suitable option.

This can be improved by highlighting how the best or most suitable option is better than the next best option.

- This is now considered a developed recommendation:
    - o this occurs when a candidate can demonstrate how the best qualities of one option outweigh the best qualities of the next best option.

Paper 1: Common, generic errors

Bullet points and lists

Unless specifically asked for, do not write lists or bullet points – a list of 15 positives and negatives will never achieve full marks, as a list cannot show 'understanding' or 'explanation' and will waste valuable time.

Writing full paragraphs for a 2 or 4-mark questions

If there are only 2 marks available, expanding a definition to include all eventualities or giving lots of examples will waste valuable time.

Only writing one identifiable element when asked for two

It is important candidates identify the 'command' word accurately: 'distinguish between the elements'. When a question asks for two elements, you must give two elements – it is impossible to gain the full marks otherwise.

Only explaining or focusing on one element in a 4- or 6-mark question

Low-scoring candidates often write full paragraphs for one element, realize they have spent too long on one question then ignore the second element.

Incorrectly identifying a minor 'command' word

For example: 'Explain why X is important to Y'. Weaker candidates may focus on the 'X' and give many examples along with a definition – X is not the 'command' word – 'explain why' and 'important to' are the 'command' words, and must be answered.

A definition of X should usually be given, and an example is a good way of showing its importance to Y. If a candidate only uses one example, this may be enough, but it must be clearly expanded, such as explaining the consequences of the example and using linking words such as 'because', 'that leads to' or 'which'.

Running out of time

It is important to allocate the correct amount of time for each question. As each full question is marked out of 20, candidates should aim for 20 minutes per question with 10 minutes then available for reading the case studies.

Not bringing a calculator to the exam

While there is no requirement to bring a calculator to any of the exams, there will be calculation questions on each paper. Two benefits of calculators are:

- it saves time when working out equations (always remember to write out your working as well)
- if a candidate is unsure of the correct formula, it is possible to run through a few options and choose the answer which has the best fit.

Not proofreading answers

It is possible to write answers that make no sense when in an exam setting. Proofreading is a valuable tool to identify glaring errors, such as incorrect formulas with improbable answers or definitions with incorrect examples.

A lack of planning, logic and preparation

It is important to structure the answers to all longer questions. Planning will allow structure, correction and thought to influence the answer and gain maximum marks. Writing a full answer without any thinking time is the single biggest cause of lost marks.

Only reading the question once

A candidate who only reads the question once will invariably begin to answer a different question, as this candidate will almost certainly not have created a plan. Every time a candidate starts a new paragraph or section, it is important to read the question again to ensure the answer still relates to the question.

Explaining/defining all elements of the question in great detail

There are only a maximum of 4 marks available for knowledge in each question, so while it is important to show understanding of the key elements, knowledge should be shown throughout the answer.

Using incorrect examples

Each question refers to a case study, and correct examples must be used. Candidates who fail to plan an answer or reread the question often link their answer to the wrong case study (or to no case study at all) and limit their marks, even though the theory and analysis is excellent.

Using undeveloped bullet points or unconnected sentences

It is almost impossible to gain 'analysis' with undeveloped and unconnected sentences. Poor answers often contain:

- short, textbook-style definitions that show an ability to remember definitions without any ability to apply the definition to an example

- lists of all the possible outcomes (e.g. the importance of X) without any attempt to apply the outcomes to the question.

Ignoring the evaluation element of the question

'Discussing' a question often requires a candidate to identify, explain and analyse limitations of a framework or theory to counter the benefits.

If there is a question that asks for the effects on a range of stakeholders, an effective method of evaluating is to rank the stakeholders that are affected the most (ranking), or considering the business environment and how that could impact on the effect.

Paper 2: Sample paper

Carla's Coats

Carla owns a chain of 10 specialist shops that sell imported, expensive, hand-made coats and accessories in country X. This business is run as a private limited company with her partner Philip, who invested the start-up capital for her first shop 15 years ago. The reputation of Carla's Coats has grown so much that they now export coats internationally and Carla is considering expanding the business.

Carla thinks that the business is successful because it focuses on a niche market, sells quality products and sells its products from shops with a luxury feel and personalized quality. However, Philip is concerned that the business spends too much money on fixed assets and cash flow has been a problem due to the fluctuating exchange rates.

Each shop employs a full-time manager and three part-time assistants who each work 20 hours a week. There is also a full-time accountant and human resources manager who looks after employee contracts.

Carla is now responsible for buying the coats and accessories and also decides on selling prices and the look of the store. When she travels abroad, she stays in upmarket hotels and has noticed that boutique hotel shops are very busy. She is considering this as an option for expansion and Philip is exploring finance options.

Appendix 1: Financial information for Carla's Coats ($m)

	2016	2017
Revenue	10	15
Cost of sales	2	3
Expenses	1	1
Capital employed	5	6

Appendix 2: Breaking news, 1 December 2018

There has been a downturn in the economy of country X due to the economy performing much worse than expected and a leading bank having declared itself bankrupt. Many businesses are worried due to the negative impact on their ability to borrow money and are unwilling to risk further investment in the domestic market.

The foreign exchange market has reacted quickly to the news and although the exchange rate is fluctuating, the currency is depreciating rapidly. The government is trying to use economic policy to stabilize the currency, however, this is likely to result in increased taxes and raised interest rates.

Question paper

1   (a) Identify and explain two reasons why brand image is important for Carla's Coats.   (8)

     (b) Consider the advantages and disadvantages of the following two ways of improving Carla's Coats' cash flow. Recommend the best option. Justify your answer.   (12)

          i.   Increasing prices

          ii. Lowering the quality of materials

2 **(a)** Explain two benefits of Carla's Coats operating as a private limited company. (8)

   (b) Carla and Philip need to raise finance if they wish to expand overseas. Consider the advantages and disadvantages of the following three sources of finance available to them. Recommend which source of finance they should choose. Justify your answer. (12)

   i. Retained profit

   ii. Issue of shares

   iii. Bank loan

3 **(a)** Identify and explain two benefits of operating in a niche market. (8)

   (b) Consider the following three channels of distribution Carla's Coats could use if it does decide to expand overseas. Recommend the best channel to keep its niche identity. Justify your answer. (12)

   i. Sell to upmarket department stores.

   ii. Open its own designer boutiques in large cities.

   iii. Open boutiques in large international hotels.

4 **(a)** Identify and explain two ways Carla's Coats could finance their expansion. (8)

   (b) Refer to Appendix 1 and any other information in the case study. Consider the wider business environment. Do you think Carla's Coats should expand overseas? Justify your answer. (12)

Mark scheme

1 **(a)** Identify and explain two reasons why brand image is important for Carla's Coats. (8)

   - **Knowledge:** award one mark for each relevant reason.

   - **Analysis:** award one mark for a relevant explanation of each reason.

   - **Application:** award two application marks for each reason.

   (b) Consider the advantages and disadvantages of the following two ways of improving Carla's Coats' cash flow. Recommend the best option. Justify your answer. (12)

		Advantages	Disadvantages
i.	Increasing prices	High cost and quality – increased prices may be acceptable	Current economic issues – customers may be cutting back
ii.	Lowering the quality of materials	Lower outlays and less risk of currency fluctuation	Brand image may be tarnished in the long run

	Knowledge, analysis and evaluation
L3	• At least 2 × Level 2 +
	• 9–10 marks for justified recommendation as to the best method to choose compared to the other methods. 7–8 marks for some limited judgment shown in recommendation as to the best method to choose.
	• At least 2 × L2 marks plus a recommendation, which is then justified.

L2	• 4–6 marks
	• Detailed discussion of the advantages and/or disadvantages of each method.
	• One L2 explanation gains 4 marks.
	• Each additional L2 explanation gains an additional mark.
L1	• 1–3 marks
	• Outline of the advantages and/or disadvantages of each method.
	• One mark for each statement.

2 **(a)** Explain two benefits of Carla's Coats operating as a private limited company. (8)

- **Knowledge:** award one mark for each relevant benefit.

- **Analysis:** award one mark for a relevant explanation of each benefit.

- **Application:** award two application marks for each benefit.

(b) Carla and Philip need to raise finance if they wish to expand overseas. Consider the advantages and disadvantages of the following three sources of finance available to them. Recommend which source of finance they should choose. Justify your answer. (12)

		Advantages	Disadvantages
i.	Retained profit	No interest or risk	May not be sufficient funds
		Readily available	May reduce dividends
ii.	Issue of shares	No repayment needed	Limited number of options as limited company
			Loss of control of the business
iii.	Bank loan	Regular amount spread over a period of time	Increased monthly costs
		Large sums potentially available	Potential cutback of borrowing opportunities due to recession

	Knowledge, analysis and evaluation
L3	• At least 2 × Level 2 +
	• 9–10 marks for justified recommendation as to the best source of finance to choose when compared to others.
	7–8 marks for some limited judgment shown in recommendation as to the best source of finance to choose.
	• At least 2 × L2 marks plus a recommendation, which is then justified.
L2	• 4–6 marks
	• Detailed discussion of the advantages and/or disadvantages of each source of finance.
	• One L2 explanation gains 4 marks.
	• Each additional L2 explanation gains an additional mark.
L1	• 1–3 marks
	• Outline of the advantages and/or disadvantages of each source of finance.
	• One mark for each statement.

3 **(a)** Identify and explain two benefits of operating in a niche market. (8)

- **Knowledge:** award one mark for each relevant benefit.
- **Analysis:** award one mark for a relevant explanation of each benefit.
- **Application:** award two application marks for each benefit.

(b) Consider the following three channels of distribution Carla's Coats could use if it does decide to expand overseas. Recommend the best channel to keep its niche identity. Justify your answer. (12)

Points could include:

		Advantages	Disadvantages
i.	Sell to upmarket department stores	Suitable locations/high footfall – increase sales	Competing brands available
ii.	Open its own designer boutiques in large cities	Control over presentation and layout	High costs
iii.	Open boutiques in large international hotels	Target market	High rental costs

	Knowledge, analysis and evaluation
L3	• At least 2 × Level 2 + • 9–10 marks for justified recommendation as to the best option to choose when compared to others. 7–8 marks for some limited judgment shown in recommendation as to the best option to choose. • At least 2 × L2 marks plus a recommendation, which is then justified.
L2	• 4–6 marks • Detailed discussion of the advantages and/or disadvantages of each option. • One L2 explanation gains 4 marks. • Each additional L2 explanation gains an additional mark.
L1	• 1–3 marks • Outline of the advantages and/or disadvantages of each option. • One mark for each statement.

4   **(a)**   Identify and explain two ways Carla's Coats could finance their expansion.   (8)

- **Knowledge:** award one mark for each relevant method.

- **Analysis:** award one mark for a relevant explanation of each method.

- **Application:** award two application marks for each method.

   (b)   Refer to Appendix 1 and any other information in the case study. Consider the wider business environment. Do you think Carla's Coats should expand overseas? Justify your answer.   (12)

Points could include:

- likely reduced demand in country X

- existing international reputation

- successful business

- could use foreign capital to buy new stock, minimizing exchange rate fluctuations.

	Knowledge, analysis and evaluation
L3	<ul><li>At least 2 × Level 2 +</li><li>9–10 marks for justified recommendation as to the best choice. 7–8 marks for some limited judgment shown in recommendation as to the best choice.</li><li>At least 2 × L2 marks plus a recommendation, which is then justified.</li></ul>
L2	<ul><li>4–6 marks</li><li>Detailed discussion of the advantages and/or disadvantages of each explanation.</li><li>One L2 explanation gains 4 marks.</li><li>Each additional L2 explanation gains an additional mark.</li></ul>
L1	<ul><li>1–3 marks</li><li>Outline of the advantages and/or disadvantages of each choice.</li><li>One mark for each statement.</li></ul>

Glossary

Above/below-the-line Above-the-line promotions are communications using mass advertising media; below-the-line advertising is more personal, such as pamphlets, stickers and brochures

Acid-test ratio Measures a company's ability to pay debt with assets that can be converted to cash within 90 days

Add value Make a product or service more valuable than the sum of the original parts

Aftersales Support and protection provided to the customer after the sale of an item

Applicant Person who has made a formal application for a job

Application form Document that applicants are required to fill out, providing information such as previous employment, education and contact details

Appreciation/depreciation Rise or fall in the price of one currency against others

Arbitration Process in which an independent referee negotiates a compromise

Asset Property owned by a person or company that is considered to have value and can be used to meet debts

Automation Application of technology to a manufacturing process or facility

Boom Period of rapid economic growth

Brand Name and/or image used to identify and distinguish a specific good, service or business from others

Brand loyalty Tendency of customers to continue buying the same brand of goods or services over competing brands

Break-even To cover all production or service costs through the sale of products or services

Building regulations Standards to be upheld when constructing buildings

Bulk buying Buying many products at once for a cheaper price than buying fewer products many times

Business cycle Measure of the total annual value of all goods and services produced by business activity in a particular country

Business failure Occurs when a business does not have the financial or other resources necessary for continued trading or production

Business objective The aim of a business, intended to guide operations

Business plan Written document that describes how a business is going to meet its objectives

Capital Money or other assets owned by a company

Cash Assets consisting of currency and/or currency equivalents that can be accessed instantly or near-instantly

Cash flow forecasts Predict monthly cash in and outflow and calculate expected cash balances every month

Chain of command Structure of an organization which dictates authority, power and responsibility at every level

Child labour Employment of children in an organization; often considered exploitative

Communication Delivery of information in a clear and correct manner

Competition Rivalry between companies providing similar products or services

Computer-aided design (CAD) Detailed and accurate drawings completed on computer programs, allowing images to be seen in 3D

Computer-aided manufacturing (CAM) Processes completed by computer-controlled robots without human operators

Consumer A person purchasing goods or services

Consumer protection laws Ensure that businesses do not make misleading, false or dangerous claims in advertising

Cost Amount to be paid to obtain a product or service

Cost-plus amount $(\frac{Total\ cost}{Total\ output})$ + percentage mark-up or fixed

Credit The capability of a consumer to obtain goods or services, based on the assurance that payment will be made in the future

Crowd funding Borrowing small amounts of capital from large numbers of investors

Current ratio Measures the ability of a business to pay its short-term debt

CV Brief summary of a person's experience and qualifications, usually submitted with a job application

Data Information collected for reference or analysis

Debenture Long-term loan with a fixed rate of interest

Debt Repayable loan, often from money lending institutions

Deficit Amount by which spending exceeds revenue

Direct mail Personalized communication to promote and provide information in a low-cost manner

Director Person in charge of an organization or department

Discrimination Unjust or prejudicial treatment on the grounds of an aspect of identity

Dismissal Ordering or allowing a person to leave a role

Distribution Making a product or service available for the consumer who requires it

Diversification Expanding or varying a range of products or services

Dividend Share of future business profits

Downsize Shed staff to make a company smaller

E-commerce Transactions made electronically over the internet

Economy/diseconomy of scale Average cost of unit production reduces as scale is increased; average cost of unit production rises because the business has grown too large

Economy State of a country or place that takes into account production and consumption of goods and services, and money

Efficiency State of achieving maximum productivity or outcome with minimum wasted product, time or expense

Embargo Total ban on certain or all goods from a particular country

Employment contract Written legal document signed and agreed by both the employee and employer

Employment law Legal controls over employment issues, impacting both employees and employers

Enterprise An organization or business

Entrepreneur Person who starts a business, taking financial risks to generate profit

Equity Stocks and shares with no fixed interest

Ethics Judgment of what is right or wrong, including the values, standards and morals that govern how society behaves

Exchange rate Value of a currency upon conversion to another

Finance Management of money

Financial motivator Payment of a wage or salary, enabling the employee to buy goods and services they need and want

Financial reward Payment of money in exchange for labour

Foreign market A market outside a company's own country

Franchise Method of business ownership in which a large company authorizes a smaller company or individual to carry out commercial activity under its name

Globalization Growth of a business allowing relocation to other countries

Government Appointed group of people with the authority to control a particular country or state

Gross Domestic Product (GDP) Total value of an economy

Gross profit margin (GPM) Shows how much profit a business makes when the cost of goods has been paid

Growth Increasing the size of a business by increasing sales and profits

Health and safety Regulations intended to protect people in the workplace

Hire purchase Paying for a product or service in instalments while continuing to use it

Import tariff Additional amount charged on goods produced outside of the country

Income statement Used to calculate, report and monitor revenues, costs and profits of a business

Industrial action Disruption of business activity by members of a trade union

Input/output Raw materials; finished products

Integration Process of achieving close coordination between two or more groups or businesses

Interest rate Cost of borrowing money

International trade Exchanging goods, services and money across national borders

Inventory Stocks of raw materials, works-in-progress and finished goods

Job production Production process used for one-off, custom products or services

Just-in-time Production method in which little or no stocks of raw materials are ordered in advance

Kaizen 'Continuous improvement' in Japanese, this is a production process based on reducing waste and improving productivity

Labour productivity $\dfrac{\text{Total output}}{\text{number of employees}}$

Lease back Raising immediate capital from non-current assets then renting them back for an agreed fee

Limited liability Legal separation between an investor's private assets and an investment – a shareholder can only lose the amount of money invested in the business

Liquidity State of having cash on hand, or assets that can be quickly sold and turned into cash

Manager Supervises activities, managers and/or other resources

Market Any location where buyers and sellers meet

Market research Tool to gather data on customer preferences, spending patterns, threats and changing market conditions

Market segmentation Divides the whole market into smaller segments, each with similar features

Marketing Creating the desire for a product or service by a supplier to entice a customer who is willing and able to buy the product

Microfinance Provision of small business loans provided within developing economies

Minimum wage Form of wage protection to ensure workers are paid above a certain amount by law

Mission statement Summary of the aims and values of a business

Multinational company (MNC) Large-scale business operating internationally but headquartered in one country

Nationalization Process of making private-sector business part of the public sector in the greater public interest

Non-financial motivator Any rewards that cannot be turned into a cash payment

Non-financial reward Any reward that cannot be turned into a cash payment

On-/off-the-job training Basic job instruction conducted inside or outside the workplace

Opportunity cost Cost associated with choosing one option over the next best alternative

Organizational structure Simple view of the chain of command

Partnership Joint ownership of a private-sector business

Penetration Setting low initial prices in an attempt to enter the market

Person specification List of skills and characteristics forming part of a job advertisement

Piece rate Pay according to the number of units produced

Pressure group Group organized to counter the negative impacts of business on the environment or society

Price elasticity Shows the responsiveness of consumer demand to a change in price

Private/public sector Businesses run for and by individuals or corporations; organizations run by the government for the public good

Profit and loss account Calculates and records total expenses and profit or loss after costs are deducted

Profit margin How much profit a business makes when all costs and expenses have been paid

Promotion Setting low prices for a short period of time to boost customer interest

Protectionism Methods by which governments protect their economies against international competition

Public expenditure Finances from tax revenues and government borrowing

Public relations (PR) Useful to repair a damaged brand or maintain a positive image through association with popular culture

Qualitative/quantitative data Includes opinions, judgments or reactions; consists of statistical data

Quality assurance/control Aims to reduce the chance of defects before they occur; testing the quality of the goods and services once they have been produced

Quota Limit on the quantity of products imported to increase demand and selling price

Raw material Items that are to be processed into products

Recession Period of economic decline

Recruitment Process of attracting and selecting employees

Redundancy The offloading of employees whose skills are outdated or no longer of use

Renewable energy Energy source in theoretically unlimited supply, as an alternative to fossil fuels

Return on capital employed (ROCE) Profitability ratio which expresses the profit of a company as a percentage of the capital employed

Salary Annual figure divided into 12 and paid monthly in return for an agreed number of hours worked per week

Sales incentive Forms of discount or loyalty scheme to incentivize continued purchasing

Sampling Selecting appropriate respondents to research exercises

Shareholder Investor in a business who has exchanged capital for a share of ownership and future business profits

Skimming Charging a high initial price to cover research and development costs in a monopolistic market

SMART Business acronym for specific, measurable, achievable, realistic and time-based

Sole trader A person who starts a business by themselves

Spill over External benefit to technological development, where benefits of a development in one business can be utilized in other sectors

Stakeholder Anyone, internally or externally, who has a vested interest in a business

Statement of financial position Records how much a business owns and owes at the end of a 12-month accounting period

Subsidy Payment to local firms to reduce production costs and selling prices

Supervisor Usually supervise employees; often recruited from within and promoted for initiative and leadership qualities

Surplus Amount of cash, goods or raw materials left over after an accounting period

SWOT analysis Business acronym meaning strengths, weaknesses, opportunities and threats

Tax Used to collect finance for public expenditure, either directly from income and profit or indirectly from spending on goods and services

Time rate Pay according to the number of hours worked

Trade union Association of employees who have similar job roles within business

Training Instruction on how to complete a job or process

Undercutting Benchmarking against a competitor price

Unlimited liability No legal distinction between the shareholder investment and personal assets – in the case of business failure the investor may lose personal assets

Venture capital Used to start business opportunities, comes from loans, savings or investors

Wage Method of payment for labour

Workforce Total employees

	Revision Period 1	Revision Period 2	Revision Period 3	Revision Period 4	Revision Period 5	Revision Period 6
Sunday						
Saturday						
Friday						
Thursday						
Wednesday						
Tuesday						
Monday						